The Incredible Indoor Games Book

Grades 1–5

Published by Instructional Fair
an imprint of

 Children's Publishing

Author: Bob Gregson
Editor: Melissa Warner Hale

 **Children's Publishing**

Published by Instructional Fair
An imprint of McGraw-Hill Children's Publishing
Copyright © 2004 McGraw-Hill Children's Publishing

All Rights Reserved • Printed in the United States of America

Limited Reproduction Permission: Permission to duplicate these materials is limited to the person for whom they are purchased. Reproduction for an entire school or school district is unlawful and strictly prohibited.

Send all inquiries to:
McGraw-Hill Children's Publishing
3195 Wilson Drive NW
Grand Rapids, Michigan 49544

The Incredible Indoor Games Book—grades 1–5
ISBN: 0-7424-1940-1

1 2 3 4 5 6 7 8 9 MAZ 08 07 06 05 04
The McGraw-Hill Companies

Table of Contents

© McGraw-Hill Children's Publishing — 0-7424-1940-1 *The Incredible Indoor Games Book*

Table of Contents (cont.)

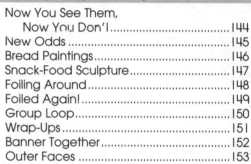
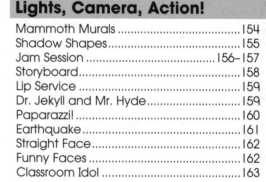

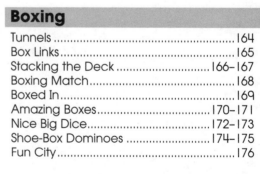
© McGraw-Hill Children's Publishing   0-7424-1940-1 *The Incredible Indoor Games Book*

Proudly Presenting

What could be more perfect than having someone tell everyone how wonderful you are? Why just dream about it?

Materials needed:

None

Room arrangement:

As is

Time:

25 minutes

Directions:

1. Players find partners. Preferably, people who don't know each other very well should pair up.

2. Partners have five minutes to trade information about things they would like others to know about their lives—hobbies; accomplishments; favorite foods, places, or things; plans for the future; and so forth.

3. Players sit in a circle (or players may stay at their desks), but partners do not sit next to each other. In turn, players stand and introduce their partners. For example: "I am very happy to say that we have an expert guitar player with us today. He likes to fish, swim, and eat chocolate-chip ice cream sundaes. May I present to you Dennis Myers!" The person introduced stands up and bows as the group applauds and cheers.

Animal, Bird, Or Fish

Players will be flying high, sailing along, and climbing the walls with this pantomime game.

Materials needed:

None

Room arrangement:

Open space

Time:

15 minutes

Directions:

1. Divide players into two teams. Teams position themselves in corners of the room opposite each other. A leader is chosen to stand in the center at an equal distance from each team.

2. Each team sends one player to the leader in the middle. The leader whispers the name of an animal, bird, or fish. If the leader says "Monkey," for example, each player runs back to his or her team to act out a monkey in pantomime.

3. When a team member guesses "monkey," the pantomiming player runs back and touches the leader, saying "Monkey!" The first player back to the leader is the winner.

4. Each team chooses a different player to perform a new pantomime. The game continues for a specified period of time or until all players have had a chance to perform a pantomime.

© McGraw-Hill Children's Publishing 0-7424-1940-1 *The Incredible Indoor Games Book*

Let's Face It

People need little or no excuse to indulge in making faces.
Here's a way to make a funny-face game.

Materials needed:

None

Room arrangement:

Open space

Time:

20 minutes

Directions:

1. Have everyone sit in a circle on the floor. The object of the game is to make the funniest face possible.

2. A short demonstration of everyone's funny face will set the tone for the game. Have players inflate cheeks, wrinkle noses, furrow eyebrows, show teeth, and so forth.

3. This game works well as a fantasy. Tell the players that a magic spell has been cast over the group, changing everyone's face. To save everyone from the spell, a funny face must pass around the entire group, person to person, until it gets back to the first person again. Then, magically, the spell will vanish!

4. After everyone has practiced making faces, the leader begins slowly changing his or her face into a funny expression and then turns slowly to a neighbor who must mirror the face.

5. The second person, after mirroring the leader's expression, changes the face as he or she turns to the third person. The third person mirrors the face, changes it, and passes it on around the entire circle.

6. The last person passes a funny face to the leader, who mirrors it and slowly changes his or her face back to normal, thus breaking the spell and saving the group.

© McGraw-Hill Children's Publishing 0-7424-1940-1 *The Incredible Indoor Games Book*

Lean and Leave

This playful mime technique teaches players an invaluable lesson in self-reliance as they become their own support system.

Materials needed:

None

Room arrangement:

Open space

Time:

10 minutes

Directions:

1. Players choose partners. The object of the game is for players to look as if they're leaning, while they are actually able to stand without support.

2. One partner leans on the shoulder of the other. The leaning player then shifts weight slightly so that he or she is actually standing alone.

3. When leaning players can lean unsupported, they say "Okay" to their partners, who move away, leaving them looking as if they were leaning on thin air.

4. After both partners have leaned alone, divide players into groups of three with two players leaning on a middle player. When the middle player moves, the two others will look as if they were chatting away and didn't notice the support was missing.

© McGraw-Hill Children's Publishing

0-7424-1940-1 *The Incredible Indoor Games Book*

Invisible Tug-of-War

Some tug-of-war games depend on pure muscle.
In this version, players must use their imagination muscles.

Materials needed:

None

Room arrangement:

Open space

Time:

10 minutes

Directions:

1. Two players are chosen to stand in front of the group and pretend they are tugging a rope back and forth—just like the original version.

2. As the two tuggers pantomime pulling the rope, one will begin to lose. When a player looks as if he or she is losing, one player from the group hops up to help out.

3. One by one, players from the group continue to add themselves to the losing team until eventually both teams are filled.

4. It may not seem possible, but as in all tug-of-war games, the stronger team will win!

10

© McGraw-Hill Children's Publishing 0-7424-1940-1 *The Incredible Indoor Games Book*

Walk My Walk

Close observation will reveal that no two people walk in the same manner.
This game investigates all walks of life.

Materials needed:

None

Room arrangement:

Open space

Time:

15 minutes

Directions:

1. Have players stand in a circle with plenty of space in the middle. Discuss the many ways in which people walk. For example, a spy might creep along on tiptoes while a fashion model walks with a studied, erect posture.

2. Players select a role with a specific kind of walk. Some ideas are:
   - tightrope walker
   - astronaut on the moon
   - window washer on a ledge
   - infant learning to walk
   - old person
   - body builder
   - marching soldier
   - circus clown
   - explorer at the North Pole

3. Each player walks across the circle several times as the group tries to guess his or her identity.

4. When someone guesses correctly, the entire group imitates the walk. The group returns to the form of the circle again to watch another player walk the walk.

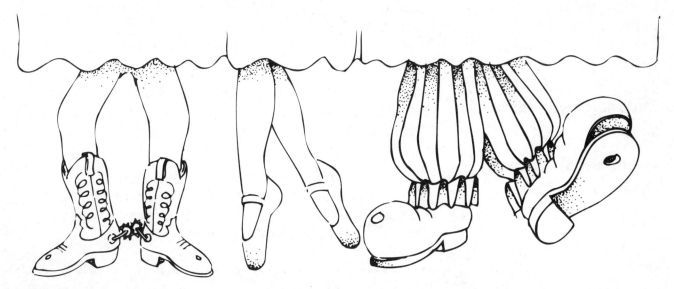

© McGraw-Hill Children's Publishing 0-7424-1940-1 *The Incredible Indoor Games Book*

Passing the Buck

Materials needed:

A glove, a beanbag, a small rubber ball, or any other small object

Room arrangement:

Open space

Time:

15 minutes

Once upon a time....

Directions:

1. Have players stand in a circle. The "buck" is any small object that can be tossed easily from player to player—a glove, a beanbag, or a rubber ball.

2. Toss the buck to a player in the circle. The person catching the buck must begin to tell a story—something made up on the spot.

3. The player holding the buck tosses it to another player who must catch it and continue the story. The story can take any form, just as long as there is an attempt to connect it to the previous player's contribution.

4. Players must not break the flow of the story no matter how fast the buck is being passed. Those who have the buck must speak—if only a few words—and then they can toss it to another player to continue the narration.

Out-of-Sight Shapes

What would happen if, without warning, you pulled a five-foot banana from your pocket and you began to peel it? Well, you can—anytime—with invisible shapes. In this game, the players' imaginations become the props.

Materials needed:

None

Room arrangement:

Open space

Time:

15 minutes

Directions:

1. Have players stand in a circle.

2. This game is a pantomime in which an individual piece of space can be squeezed, squashed, twisted, or rolled into any imaginable object. To begin, quietly pull a chunk of invisible space out of your pocket or from behind your back. Continue to expand it into a large pretend object, such as a fishing pole or an oversized baseball bat. Transform your invisible object into another form, and then pass it along to the next person.

3. Each player should take about 30 seconds to transform the shape from a ball to a balloon to a hat—anything! After finishing, each player passes the shape along to the next player.

4. When the invisible shape gets back to you, treat it carefully in order to maintain its mysteriousness. Gently squeeze it back into a small ball and put it away so that it can be used again at some other time.

© McGraw-Hill Children's Publishing

0-7424-1940-1 *The Incredible Indoor Games Book*

Close Calls

This game is based on the old familiar game of Telephone, but you won't find these variations in any phone book.

Materials needed:

None

Room arrangement:

Open space

Time:

15 minutes

Directions:

1. In the oldest form of Telephone, players sit in a straight line while the person at one end whispers a brief message to the next person.

2. The second player whispers the message to the third person who, in turn, whispers it to the fourth person.

3. The story makes its way down the line to the end. The final person repeats the message aloud. It will likely bare little resemblance to the original. You can count on at least one player distorting it dramatically.

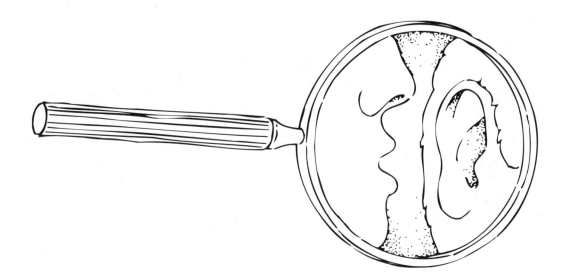

Variations:

- Gather players in a circle. Instead of passing a single message around in one direction, try passing two messages in opposite directions.

- Have many people pass messages at the same time. Have players sit in a circle and count off alternately—one and two. To begin, each "one" whispers a message to the "two" on the right. Next, the "twos" pass the messages along, so that many messages are being passed at once. The messages go around the entire circle until they return to the originators. Players tell their messages in both the original and altered versions.

© McGraw-Hill Children's Publishing 0-7424-1940-1 *The Incredible Indoor Games Book*

Real-Life Drama

"Real life is the stuff of drama." Or is it "Drama is the stuff of real life"?
In this game, dramatic real-life experiences become dramatic dramas.

Materials needed:

None

Room arrangement:

Open space

Time:

30 minutes

Directions:

1. Players sit in a circle on the floor and each tells the most interesting, dramatic thing that has happened to her or to him—getting lost, playing in an exciting ball game, rescuing an ailing bird, being in an accident, riding in a parade—something that was exciting, scary, or unusual. Players should tell stories they feel comfortable sharing with the group. Set a one-minute time limit for each player's story.

2. After everyone has told a story, divide the groups into smaller groups of five or six. Each group selects several elements from each person's story that can be combined into a short skit. Encourage imaginative combinations, such as picking up a baby bird while crossing the goal line for the winning touchdown.

3. Each group takes a turn to perform its skit for everyone.

14

© McGraw-Hill Children's Publishing

0-7424-1940-1 *The Incredible Indoor Games Book*

Now the News

After you've played Telephone, you know how stories change dramatically as they are passed from person to person. In this game, players pretend they are on-the-spot reporters adding to a news story as it unfolds without any planning.

Materials needed:

None

Room arrangement:

Chairs in a circle

Time:

15 minutes

Directions:

1. Get everyone positioned comfortably in a circle. The object of this game is for each player to add three words to a single story as it is passed around the group. The three words should help describe an incredible news story.

2. Begin the story slowly. For example, the first player might say, "Late last night…" the second player might add "…a green monster…" while the next player adds "…ate New York." If someone gets stuck and can't think of something, come back later. It is important to keep the game moving along from player to player.

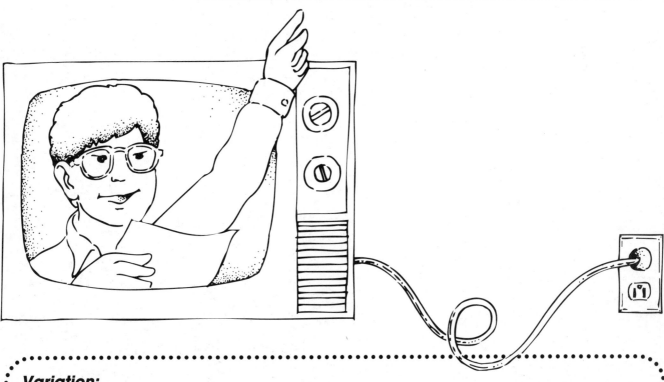

Variation:

Select a simple object such as a paper bag, a key, or a piece of string— anything small that can be passed around. As it is being passed around the group, have each player add three words to its life story. Allow each person's imagination to unravel as the object's family, friends, and travels are discussed.

© McGraw-Hill Children's Publishing 0-7424-1940-1 *The Incredible Indoor Games Book*

Outright Lie

This game should turn up the most inventive and believable storyteller in the group. Everyone will get a chance to tell the most far-out story in as truthful a manner as possible.

Materials needed:

A key, a ring, a pencil, or any other small object

Room arrangement:

As is

Time:

25 minutes

Directions:

1. Select a small object such as a key, a ring, or a pencil. Players should be seated in their usual places and pass the object from player to player.

2. As the object is passed around the room, each player must come up with an incredible story or fantasy to tell the rest of the group. For example, if a key is selected, the stories might sound like this: "This key unlocks a treasure worth more than Fort Knox, a treasure located 14 miles below the surface of the Atlantic Ocean." Or: "This key saved the life of a man when it stopped a bullet while he was fighting in a war."

3. After everyone has finished, ask the group members which lie they enjoyed the most. The most entertaining storyteller may have the dubious honor of being the least-trusted person in the group.

© McGraw-Hill Children's Publishing 0-7424-1940-1 *The Incredible Indoor Games Book*

Fact or Fiction?

In this game, style is just as important as content. Players tell plausible fictions or outrageous facts while others try to guess which is which.

Materials needed:

None

Room arrangement:

Open space

Time:

20 minutes

Directions:

1. Have players sit in a circle. The object of the game is to try to tell a true story that sounds like a lie or a lie that sounds like a true story.

2. Players take turns relating true or imaginary information about themselves or their families. The leader should set the tone by giving an example: "I have a pet swan. My mother always sneezes because she's allergic to its feathers."

3. After each turn the group must judge whether the story is fact or fiction. If a person is lying and the group thinks that it is the truth—or if the person is telling the truth and the group thinks that it is a lie—that person wins. However, if the person is telling the truth or a lie, and the group guesses correctly, the group wins. Remember, truth is often stranger than fiction, so lying isn't always necessary.

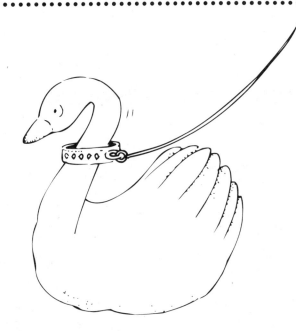

Variation:

Do the same project in writing and exchange papers.

© McGraw-Hill Children's Publishing 0-7424-1940-1 *The Incredible Indoor Games Book*

Coming and Going

You never know if someone is happy to see you or is just faking it. When the person goes, you hope she or he leaves happy and not angry. This game will make things even more confusing as you invent a few new greetings and farewells.

Materials needed:

None

Room arrangement:

Open space

Time:

10–15 minutes

Directions:

1. Have students list ways in which they greet friends and family members—from "I'm home!" to "Hi ya!" to "Hey, how's it going?" Then list ways in which people say good-bye ("See you around," or "Catch ya later"). We greet people differently during a holiday or anniversary. In what ways do people in other cultures greet each other? Explore hand gestures or other salutations.

2. Players invent their own ways to enter and leave a room, with their own greetings and gestures. This is not a serious activity, so players can be as silly as they would like and might invent their own words for "hello" and "good-bye."

3. When everyone is ready, each player has a chance to make an entrance and exit using his or her new greeting.

4. Players vote on the greeting that seems the most successful, and everyone tries it.

Transformations

With this game, the leader can easily change a group of players into a jumbo jet.

Materials needed:

None

Room arrangement:

Open space

Time:

15 minutes

Directions:

1. Divide the group into two teams. The object of the game is for players to form as quickly as possible into human representations of whatever you describe.

2. Call out the name of an object. Team members must then arrange themselves in that shape. For example, if you say "Helicopter," players must decide how they will link together into rotors, cockpit, and landing gear. Other ideas for transformations are suspension bridge, ship, cathedral, capitol dome, tree, waterfall, truck, bus, and skyscraper.

© McGraw-Hill Children's Publishing 0-7424-1940-1 *The Incredible Indoor Games Book*

Living Clay

Over the years, artists have used some pretty unusual stuff to make works of art. Here's an art project in which the players become the medium.

Materials needed:

None

Room arrangement:

Open space

Time:

15 minutes

Directions:

1. Each person selects a partner. One person becomes a blob of clay, and the other becomes the sculptor.

2. The sculptor molds and forms the human clay into any shape possible without hurting the clay. Arms can be turned, legs can be bent, heads can be tipped, and faces can be pushed into strange expressions. The clay may resist any unreasonable positions.

3. When the sculptor is finished, the creation may be put on exhibit. After the exhibit, the sculptor and sculpture should switch places.

Variation:

Divide the entire group into smaller groups of five or six. One person in each group is selected as the sculptor and the others become the clay. The sculptor uses all the others, intertwining limbs and bodies, to form a single sculpture. For a finale, make the world's largest living sculpture using the entire group as clay.

© McGraw-Hill Children's Publishing 0-7424-1940-1 *The Incredible Indoor Games Book*

Human Machine Company

Machines are useless unless each part is functioning properly. In this activity, groups of players become machines, with each player taking the role of one machine part.

Materials needed:

None

Room arrangement:

Open space

Time:

15 minutes

Directions:

1. Have players form into groups of eight or ten. Each group agrees on a single machine to portray, such as a washing machine, blender, helicopter, or lawn mower—anything with moving parts. The object of the activity is to give an impression of a machine and how all the parts work together.

2. One by one, each player pretends to be a machine part and joins the machine. For example, if everyone decides to make a car, then one chugs and shakes to make the engine, another bends over to become the trunk, another stretches arms to become the windshield, and yet another moves arms to become windshield wipers.

3. After the machine has been completed, see how well the parts work together. Have each part of the machine add a sound; see what different sounds there are when the machine is running at top speed and then at a very slow speed.

4. After each group creates an impression of a specific machine, have the groups reassemble into a totally imaginary invention.

© McGraw-Hill Children's Publishing

0-7424-1940-1 *The Incredible Indoor Games Book*

Talk Show

Did you ever dream that you were a very famous person from television or the movies? This game lets people forget about their own personalities and become the famous people they dream about.

Materials needed:

None

Room arrangement:

As is

Time:

30 minutes

Directions:

1. Choose three players to be the performers. One of them will be a very confused talk show host who does not know the identities of the day's guests. The other two players will be famous guests. The rest of the group becomes the live studio audience.

2. Two players leave the room in order to choose two famous characters to portray. Characters can be from real life or fiction, alive or dead, and should be familiar to all or most of the group. It is usually helpful if the two have some common interest such as music, sports, or politics so that they can carry on a conversation.

3. The two players rejoin the host at the front of the group. The host should begin the show, trying to pretend like he or she knows what's going on. The host might say "Welcome to *Daily Talk*. Today we have two very distinguished guests with us. These guests need no introduction, because everyone knows of their great accomplishments." Then the host should turn to one of the guests and ask a very general question, like "What have you been up to lately?"

4. The two guests begin to have a conversation as if they are two famous people meeting on a television talk show. Warn players not to give each other away with names.

5. The host must try to guess the identities of the two guests, without offending them by calling them by the wrong names! The host may ask questions to try to determine their identities. Or, the host can open the floor to members of the studio audience, who can ask the guests questions. But remember, nobody wants to admit they don't know such famous guests! So, they should not ask questions like "Are you George Washington?" Instead, the question might be "Do you get splinters from your wooden teeth?" If the guess is wrong and the player is not George Washington, he or she might answer, "I don't have to use them since my teeth are all real."

6. The host and audience continue to ask questions until the host knows the identities of the characters (or until a specified time limit runs out). The host then declares that time is up and thanks his or her guests by name for appearing on the show that day. If the host calls someone by an incorrect name, then the audience gets a chance to guess.

© McGraw-Hill Children's Publishing 0-7424-1940-1 *The Incredible Indoor Games Book*

Lip Sync

Have you ever seen a movie that was made in a different language and the English words were dubbed in? If you have, you know that the mouth movements don't always match the words. In this game, the actors pantomime, the dubbers supply the dialogue, and lots of surprises occur.

Materials needed:

None

Room arrangement:

Open space

Time:

30 minutes

Directions:

1. Four people play at a time. Two are actors and two are dubbers. The rest of the group is the audience.

2. The two actors decide on a real-life drama that includes two characters and a situation. For example:

   • two people on vacation when their car runs out of gas

   • a person smoking a cigarette in a no-smoking section and a nonsmoker

   • a person in a restaurant who keeps changing her or his order and an impatient server

   • a telemarketer trying to sell someone a kangaroo

3. The actors and the dubbers work out a very rough plot outline without actually deciding on the dialogue.

4. The actors play out the performance in pantomime. Offstage, the dubbers fill in the words. As the performance progresses, the actors and dubbers eventually affect each other and spontaneous things begin to happen.

5. Switch actors and dubbers frequently. Everyone likes to be onstage so try to give everyone a chance to be an actor or dubber at least once.

© McGraw-Hill Children's Publishing   0-7424-1940-1 *The Incredible Indoor Games Book*

In the Manner of the Adverb

Here's a pantomime guessing game that will have everyone hamming it up. Some players do pantomime interpretations of adverbs while others try to guess the words.

Materials needed:

None

Room arrangement:

As is

Time:

20–30 minutes

Directions:

1. One person selected as "It" leaves the room.

2. The players remaining in the room select an adverb such as *merrily, nervously, warmly,* and so on. The adverb should not be too obvious or too obscure but difficult enough to cause some thinking.

3. After a word has been agreed on, the person waiting outside the room can come back and try to guess the word by asking members of the group to perform an action to demonstrate the adverb. For example, he or she might say, "Shake hands in the manner of the adverb" or "Walk in the manner of the adverb."

4. The person who is "It" keeps on asking for demonstrations until he or she guesses the word. If it becomes too difficult to guess the word and all possibilities are exhausted, you or the players can give clues to keep the game moving along.

© McGraw-Hill Children's Publishing   0-7424-1940-1 *The Incredible Indoor Games Book*

World Premiere

Materials needed:

Objects found in
the room

Room arrangement:

Open space

Time:

30 minutes

Directions:

1. Divide players into groups of five.

2. Discuss with everyone the situations to be used as the basis for each group's skit. Suggest something whimsical. For example,

   - cave people fixing dinner
   - astronauts on an expedition to Mars encountering Martians
   - three fish, a frog, and a turtle living in a polluted river
   - an updated fairy tale such as "Goldilocks and the Three Bears" or "The Tortoise and the Hare"

3. After each group has a rough outline, have players find objects in the room as props. The objects can be used as themselves or as substitutes for something else. For example, a broom can be used to sweep or it can become the oar of a boat or an electric guitar.

4. As players organize their productions, rearrange furniture to make an impromptu stage.

5. When everyone is ready, add a playful air of exaggerated seriousness as you introduce the skits. Allow five minutes for each improvised world premiere. As an added touch, have each group take a bow as the rest cheer them on.

© McGraw-Hill Children's Publishing

What's Your Sign Language?

We all know we are able to communicate when we speak the same language, but speaking isn't the only way we communicate. We communicate through gestures and expressions as well. This is a game that begins to invent a new language—without saying a word!

Materials needed:

None

Room arrangement:

Seated in a circle

Time:

20 minutes

Directions:

1. Discuss with the entire group ways that we communicate without language. How do we say "hello" or "good-bye" (waving our hands) or how do we say "yes" and "no" (nodding or shaking our heads)? We point our fingers to direct attention or gesture to have people follow us.

2. Divide players into groups of three.

3. Each group of three players writes a short sentence that describes something the players enjoy doing ("I like playing baseball in the summer") or describes an aspect of their school ("Our school has a long hallway").

4. Each group must come up with new gestures, or sign language, for the words in its sentence. Gestures can be silly, like rubbing your head or shaking your foot, but each group member must agree on the movements.

5. Each group takes a turn performing its gestures in unison. Everyone else can guess the sentence (which might be rather difficult). After every group has performed, try playing some music and have the entire group "shake, rattle, and roll" their new language.

Keyboarding

Usually, only one person at a time uses a computer keyboard. But in this game, each player has a key role.

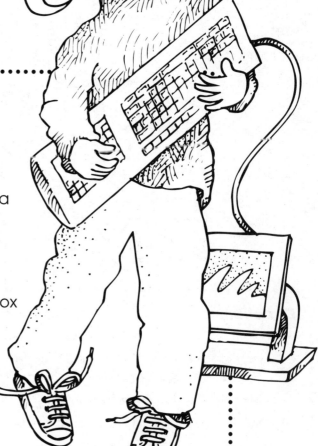

Materials needed:

None

Room arrangement:

Open space

Time:

15 minutes

Directions:

1. Gather players in a circle. Each player represents a letter in the alphabet, A through Z. If there are more players than there are letters, one can become a number, another a period, and another a backspace for correcting mistakes.

2. Find or create a sentence or paragraph that uses all the letters, numbers, and punctuation marks represented by the players. For example, "The quick brown fox jumps over the lazy dog."

3. Then, create a keyboarding rhythm for everyone to follow. Everyone claps hands, stamps a foot once, and punches the key by raising a hand in the air. Clap-stamp-punch, clap-stamp-punch—alternating right and left hands and feet.

4. Write the sentence(s) on the board for everyone to see during the game. The object is to type out the entire phrase using the proper keys without missing a beat. When the rhythm begins and everyone punches the air, the person with the first letter calls out "T!" When everyone punches the air again, the person with the next letter calls out "H!" On the next punch, the player calls out "E!" When a space between words is reached, everyone calls out together "Space!" If a mistake is made, just keep going, unless there is a person acting as the backspace key to call out "Backspace!"

© McGraw-Hill Children's Publishing 0-7424-1940-1 *The Incredible Indoor Games Book*

Rain Game

In the Rain Game, players create the sound of a rainstorm in the dry and cozy comfort of the indoors.

Materials needed:

None

Room arrangement:

Open space

Time:

10 minutes

Directions:

1. Players stand in a circle. The leader starts by rubbing his or her hands together. The person to the right of the leader joins in, then the next person to the right, then the next, until everyone is active.

2. When all are rubbing their hands, the leader starts a new sound—fingers snapping. The rain is gaining in intensity. Each player must continue to rub hands until it is his or her turn to snap fingers.

3. After finger snapping has gone all the way around, the leader begins the next sound—hands slapping thighs.

4. Finally, the crescendo of the rainstorm—hands slapping thighs plus foot stomping, is added.

5. To end the rainstorm, completely reverse the activities. The last sound to be passed is the silence as each person, one by one, stops rubbing his or her hands together.

© McGraw-Hill Children's Publishing

Dum Dum Da Da

This is a sound and movement game that can be continually enhanced by those playing it. The instructions may appear complicated, but don't get scared—it's a simple rhythm game.

Materials needed:

None

Room arrangement:

Open space

Time:

15 minutes

Directions:

1. Have all players sit on the floor in a circle with their legs crossed, each knee touching the knee of the next person. Sing or chant "Dum dum da da" to a tune or rhythm of your choice, like "Twinkle, Twinkle Little Star."

2. Repeat "dum dum da da" eight times with everyone in the group singing along.

3. After you've practiced the song with the group, you're ready to add some movements. On "dum dum," have players slap their own knees twice. On "da da," each player taps the knee of the person on the right. On the next "dum dum," players slap their own knees twice again, and finally on "da da," each taps the knee of the person on the left.

4. After everyone has mastered these movements, other movements can be added. Again on "dum dum," players slap their knees twice the regular way. On "da da," players cross right arm over left and slap the right knee with the left hand and then slap the left knee with the right hand.

5. Next, try inventing some of your own movements. On "dum dum," clap hands twice; on "da da," kick legs straight in toward the center of the circle or add arm movements, head movements, and whole-body movements.

6. The game continues until players feel they have explored as many movement possibilities as they can.

© McGraw-Hill Children's Publishing 0-7424-1940-1 *The Incredible Indoor Games Book*

Ripples

This follow-the-leader game is as beautiful to watch as it is fun to play. It resembles those elaborate movie musicals with lots of dancers creating ever-changing geometric patterns.

Materials needed:

None

Room arrangement:

Open space

Time:

10 minutes

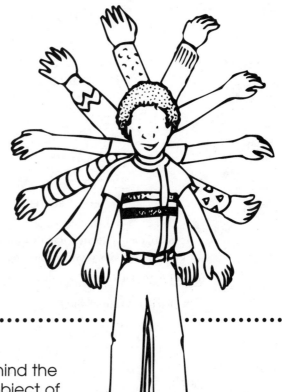

Directions:

1. Gather the group into a single line behind the person chosen to be the leader. The object of the game is to follow the movements of the person directly in front of you rather than following the leader directly.

2. The leader begins a motion that is passed down the line. If the leader raises his or her arm, the second person follows the leader, the third person follows the second, the fourth person follows the third, and so on. The leader does not walk around the room but rather moves arms and legs; bends, leans, and so on, in place.

3. After players have done this a few times, divide the group into two lines, with two leaders facing each other. In this version, the second leader mirrors the movements of the first leader. You tell leaders when to switch roles.

4. For the spectacular finale, divide the group into four groups with four leaders facing each other in a big X pattern. Two leaders initiate moves while the other two leaders follow. This version can be used with music to create a spectacular dance performance.

© McGraw-Hill Children's Publishing 0-7424-1940-1 *The Incredible Indoor Games Book*

Johnny Went to Sleep

This is a sound and movement game that, like an old-fashioned slapstick comedy, builds and builds until it's truly a ridiculous sight.

Materials needed:

None

Room arrangement:

Open space

Time:

10 minutes

Directions:

1. Players stand in a circle. The first player begins by saying "Johnny went to sleep." The rest of the group answers, "How did Johnny go to sleep?" The leader then says "Johnny went to sleep like this, like this," repeating a small gesture such as nodding the head or twisting the wrist. The rest of the group mimics the gesture and answers "Like this, like this."

2. The entire group continues to repeat the gesture as the next player in line says "Johnny went to sleep," and the others respond as before. The second player adds another gesture to the first, so that now there are two movements to keep going.

3. The game continues around the circle with each player adding a gesture.

4. By the end of the game, the entire group should be a foot-wiggling, eye-blinking, head-shaking, nose-twitching mess. Try to add as many gestures as possible before the game totally falls apart. Since it is difficult to do more than ten gestures at once, you may not get to everyone in the group, but the challenge is to see how far you do get. Start off slowly with small things, such as toes and fingers, and work up to the bigger things, such as arms and legs. Whatever happens, don't get too shook up!

© McGraw-Hill Children's Publishing 0-7424-1940-1 *The Incredible Indoor Games Book*

Thumper

Thumper is a traditional children's game and you've probably played it at some time in your life. Since it's a game that involves memory, groups of eight or ten players work best.

Materials needed:

None

Room arrangement:

Open space

Time:

15 minutes

Directions:

1. Have the players form groups of eight to ten. Have each group sit on the floor in a circle.

2. Each person must invent a sound and a movement—shaking the head while whistling, winking an eye while snapping fingers, and so on. Have each person demonstrate his or her sound and movement while other group members follow along so that all players will know each other's sound and movement.

3. To play, the first person slaps thighs and asks, "What's the name of the game?" The rest of the group, also slapping thighs, responds "Thumper!" The leader, still slapping, asks, "How do you play?" The group, still slapping, answers, "You thump!"

4. Immediately after this beginning ritual, the group begins the cadence of slapping thighs twice and then snapping fingers—first the left and then the right hand. While the rest of the group snaps the fingers of their left hands, the leader does his or her own sound and movement. While the groups snaps the fingers of their right hands, the leader does the sound and movement of another person in the group. This passes responsibility for carrying on the game to that person. Everyone slaps thighs. Then the person whose sound and movement the leader has selected repeats his or her own and then the sound and movement of someone else while the rest of the group snaps fingers. The sound and movement is thus passed around the circle from person to person.

5. If someone fails to recognize his or her own sound and movement, the game begins again. The object of the game is to see how long players can keep it up before making a mistake.

© McGraw-Hill Children's Publishing 0-7424-1940-1 *The Incredible Indoor Games Book*

Conducting

A conductor leading an orchestra uses a form of sign language in order to communicate ideas to musicians. This game requires a similar type of nonverbal expression.

Materials needed:

None

Room arrangement:

As is

Time:

20 minutes

Directions:

1. As a group, decide on some simple hand signals that refer to a specific sound. For example, raising a hand in the air might mean a high-pitched "ooh"; making a fist may refer to a deep growl; wiggling a finger could be associated with a "boo"; and showing all ten fingers might represent a shout of "hooray!"

2. Begin with four simple sounds and signals. Practice them with the group so that when the signal is given, everyone recognizes it immediately and makes the sound. Do this repeatedly, changing the order of the sound signals each time.

3. After everyone has tried each sound a few times, divide players into four groups—one for each sound.

4. Conduct the group using several signals at once so that two or three groups will be making sounds simultaneously. Add a gesture that will suggest loudness and softness. For example, raise one hand to produce a sound. Slowly lower the hand to soften the sound.

5. As the group begins to follow directions and signals with more accuracy, add more signals and sounds.

© McGraw-Hill Children's Publishing 0-7424-1940-1 *The Incredible Indoor Games Book*

Soundings

Despite the fact that we talk all the time, few of us have explored the incredible variations that are possible with our voices.

Materials needed:

None

Room arrangement:

Open space

Time:

20 minutes

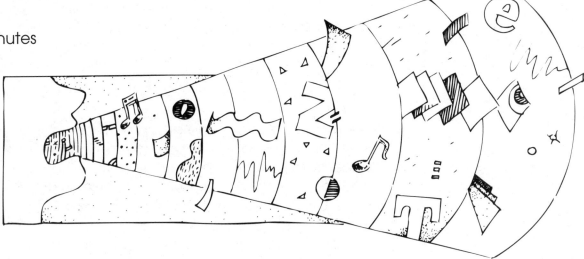

Directions:

1. Players sit in a circle and clear throats, ready for action. The object of this activity is to see how many different sounds can be made with just voices.

2. Players take turns saying their names as quickly and as slowly as they can, adding voice variations. Players can come up with some remarkable sounds if they draw out the pronunciation of their names for fifteen or twenty seconds.

3. Players close eyes. Start by making a sound—tongue click, hum, beep, whistle, or whatever—and passing it along. The sound is passed from player to player as quickly as possible. Try passing several different sounds along at the same time.

4. Open eyes and ask players to imitate a sound—birds in the forest, waves breaking on the beach, traffic sounds, musical instruments, and so forth. Ask players if anyone has a special sound he or she would like the group to guess.

5. Have small groups of players sing the tunes but not the words of familiar songs, using not their singing voices but unusual sounds. How would three frogs sound singing the tune to "Row, Row, Row Your Boat"?

© McGraw-Hill Children's Publishing 0-7424-1940-1 *The Incredible Indoor Games Book*

Creating Silence

Although this game has a sound foundation, it is actually about silence. Sound and silence, just like other opposites, need each other in order to be understood and appreciated. Players might think that they are playing only with sound, but they are also playing with the absence of it.

Materials needed:

None

Room arrangement:

Open space

Time:

10 minutes

Directions:

1. Everyone sits quietly in a circle. You begin by making two sounds, "beep—hum," leaving a short silence between them. Ask players what they heard. They will probably answer "beep—hum" without recognizing the silence. Try again, leaving a longer gap of silence. Explain that silence separates and defines the two sounds just as the two sounds define or "frame" the silence.

2. To demonstrate, have the group hum one continuous sound for 30 seconds. The sound was defined by the silence before and after. Have everyone hum again for 30 seconds, but this time break it with a short silence every 10 seconds. Try adding a few more silences to the 30-second hum to create a rhythm. Keep adding silences until the sound almost disappears.

3. Have everyone close his or her eyes and be as silent as possible. Instruct players to add a sound to the silence, slowly filling it up. Players make random sounds with their voices—beeps, hums, whistles, clicks, and so forth—in order to change the shape of the silence. When the silence becomes filled with an

© McGraw-Hill Children's Publishing   0-7424-1940-1 *The Incredible Indoor Games Book*

Syllable Symphony

Here's an auditory puzzle that takes a good ear to piece together.

Materials needed:

None

Room arrangement:

Open space

Time:

15 minutes

Directions:

1. Everyone sits in a circle. One person is chosen to be "It" and goes out of the room. The rest of the group picks one word with three or more syllables, such as the word *De-cem-ber*.

2. Count off by syllables so that each person has part of the word—the first person would be *de*; the second person, *cem*; the third, *ber*; the fourth, *de* again; and so on. Pick a song with a simple melody such as "Row, Row, Row Your Boat" or "Yankee Doodle."

3. Each person sings his or her syllable to the tune of the song. For example, one would sing "De, de, de, de, de," another would sing "Cem, cem, cem, cem, cem," and the rest "Ber, ber, ber, ber, ber," all together to the same melody.

4. The person who is "It" comes back into the room. He or she must listen carefully as the group is singing and try to piece together the word.

© McGraw-Hill Children's Publishing   0-7424-1940-1 *The Incredible Indoor Games Book*

The Minister's Cat

The human qualities of cats have always fascinated people. Although the origin of this game is not certain, it was no doubt inspired by a rather colorful feline.

Materials needed:

None

Room arrangement:

Open space

Time:

10 minutes

The principal's horse

Directions:

1. This game is fun if players sit in a circle on the floor. The object of the game is to provide adjectives describing the minister's cat. Each new adjective must begin with a different letter of the alphabet. "The minister's cat is an angry cat." The next person would have to use a word that starts with B and might say "The minister's cat is a beautiful cat," and so on.

2. It is helpful, and lots more fun, if players tap out a soft rhythm on their knees throughout the game. Each person should be prepared with a new word when his or her turn comes, so the rhythm is not broken. The rhythm emphasizes different parts of the sentence: "The MIN-ister's CAT is a CRANK-y Cat." Speed up or slow down the rhythm, depending on how well the group is doing.

© McGraw-Hill Children's Publishing 0-7424-1940-1 *The Incredible Indoor Games Book*

Jamackwack

In darkest regions of Wackidonia lives the little-known Jamackwack bird. The Jamackwack bird cannot see or fly and prefers to walk backward! As you can probably guess, this is a unique bird, seen only on the rarest occasions—except when playing this game.

Materials needed:

None

Room arrangement:

Open space

Time:

15 minutes

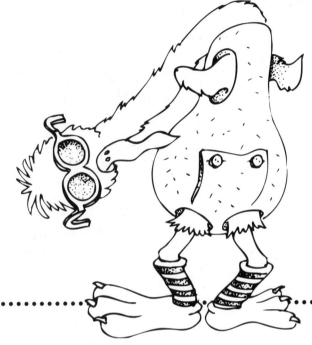

Directions:

1. Divide the group into two teams. One team will impersonate the famous Jamackwack birds. Since the Jamackwacks only walk in reverse, players must bend over, hold onto their ankles, close their eyes, and walk backward. The other team creates a corral by standing hand in hand in a circle around the birds so that they can't escape. But, there is an open gate, a place where two players do not hold hands.

2. The Jamackwacks must find the opening in order to get out. When a Jamackwack discovers the opening, he or she starts to yell, "Wack! Wack! Wack!" to the other Jamackwacks. The other Jamackwacks, hearing the calls, will discover where the opening is and begin to make their way to the gate by following the yells.

3. Meanwhile, the people in the circle around the birds can do nothing to stop their escape except drown out the calls of the free Jamackwacks by singing a song ("Old MacDonald," "Row, Row, Row Your Boat," or whatever) as loudly as possible. The more birds that escape, the louder everyone has to sing.

4. When every Jamackwack has finally found his or her way out of the corral, those playing birds and those playing the corral switch roles. There are no winners or losers in this game, but it is very amusing to observe how the rarely seen Jamackwack birds behave.

© McGraw-Hill Children's Publishing 0-7424-1940-1 *The Incredible Indoor Games Book*

Zink Vortex

Named after Thomas Zink, infamous player and inventor of fun, the Zink Vortex is an elegant exercise in "loco" motion.

Materials needed:

None

Room arrangement:

Open space

Time:

5–10 minutes

Directions:

1. Pick a song to sing while playing this game. Choose a standard that everyone knows such as "Row, Row, Row Your Boat," "The Farmer in the Dell," or "Yankee Doodle"—something that can be performed with gusto.

2. Join the players in holding hands in a circle.

3. Release your left hand and begin to coil inward, slowly leading the players on your right hand in a spiral inside the circle.

4. When you reach the center of the circle, turn around and begin to lead players in a reverse spiral. Players following the inside spiral will pass outgoing players walking in the opposite direction.

5. To end, the entire group re-forms into a circle and finishes the song.

Knock, Knock, Knock

Although we may not be aware of it, sound shapes our perception of things. This game tests players' abilities and sensitivities to decipher the sounds around them.

Materials needed:

None

Room arrangement:

As is

Time:

10 minutes

Directions:

1. Players close their eyes. The leader quietly moves around the room and chooses an object or thing and clearly knocks on it three times—moving away as silently as possible so as not to give away his or her location.

2. Once a distance from the object, the leader instructs players to open their eyes. The leader calls on players one by one to name the object until the object is discovered.

3. After the game has been played several times, discuss how sounds differ from one material to another and how environments can muffle or distort sounds.

© McGraw-Hill Children's Publishing 0-7424-1940-1 *The Incredible Indoor Games Book*

Opposites Attract

Contrary to public opinion, you've got to be sharp to be really silly. This game takes some reverse psychology.

Materials needed:

None

Room arrangement:

Open space

Time:

10 minutes

Directions:

1. Arrange players in a circle. To begin, the leader stands in the center of the group.

2. The leader does something and everyone else has to do the exact opposite.

   For example:

   • Leader pulls his or her left ear and others pull their right ears.

   • Leader stands on his or her right foot and others stand on their left feet.

   • Leader opens his or her mouth and others close their mouths.

   • Leader turns left and others turn right.

3. Allow others to be the leader—possibly one who first makes a mistake. Or, eliminate players who make mistakes until one winner remains (this will prolong the game). This person can be the next leader.

© McGraw-Hill Children's Publishing 0-7424-1940-1 *The Incredible Indoor Games Book*

No, No, No!

In this game, everyone agrees to change a sentence just a bit, until the sentence makes little or no sense. Rather than making things clearer, each player gets a turn to make things more ridiculous in a more authoritative way.

Materials needed:

None

Room arrangement:

As is

Time:

15 minutes

Directions:

1. Players can be seated in chairs or in a circle on the floor. The object of the game is to pass a sentence around from person to person, changing one word each time.

2. To play, the first person begins with a simple sentence. For example: "The dog went to sleep."

3. The next person responds in an outraged tone, "No, no, no! The hippo went to sleep," changing only one word. The next person might say, "No, no, no! The hippo went to Pittsburgh." And so on.

4. Allow only a few seconds for thought. Have a time limit. If someone gets stuck, go on to the next person. Encourage the most unusual word combinations—and don't worry if they don't make sense.

Because

This game is for those who think they know all the answers.

Materials needed:

None

Room arrangement:

As is

Time:

15 minutes

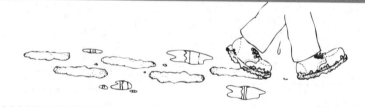

Directions:

1. Players can be seated as they are or on the floor in a circle. The first player must describe an everyday situation in a simple way. For example: "My shoes are muddy."

2. The next person must tell the reason why. For example: "Because it's raining outside."

3. The third player must figure out a probable effect. For example: "And my footprints are all over the floor."

4. The next player begins with a simple description and the game follows with the next two responses. Encourage players to state cause and effect rapidly and not to worry about coming up with the best answer. The key is spontaneity.

Something Bad About Something Good

In this game everyone will investigate the bad qualities of some very nice things.

Materials needed:

None

Room arrangement:

As is

Time:

25 minutes

Directions:

1. Ask everyone to think about a favorite thing. It could be a person, a place, or an object.

2. Now, have everyone think of its bad qualities. What are the things that it cannot do? What are its limitations?

3. Give each person a turn to describe a favorite thing in unfavorable terms without telling what the thing is. Encourage players to make their things sound as awful as they can without lying. For example, if the thing is a balloon, a player might say "You can't sit on it. You have to be careful that it does not explode. It doesn't last long, and it is impossible to keep in a room full of porcupines."

4. If everyone is stumped and the player has run out of bad things, suggest giving one "good" clue. The first person to guess correctly gets the next chance to describe something. Try, however, to give everyone at least one turn.

Variation:

This game can be played in reverse by describing the good points of bad things.

© McGraw-Hill Children's Publishing

0-7424-1940-1 *The Incredible Indoor Games Book*

Alphabet Travels

The more we learn to enjoy words to express ourselves, the more we are motivated to acquire skills that will help us use language in a variety of ways. This alliteration game should be played for the pure pleasure of playing.

Materials needed:

None

Room arrangement:

Open space

Time:

15 minutes

My name is Kris
I'm going to Kansas
to kick kangaroos.

Directions:

1. Players can be seated in chairs or on the floor in a circle. The object of the game is to go through the entire alphabet, each player making a sentence using as many words as possible with a particular letter. It is helpful to give each person a letter beforehand so everyone has time to prepare. For fairness, leave out the letter X.

2. Each sentence must start with "I am going to…" and then name a place and a reason. For example:

   • First player: "I am going to Alabama to avoid angry alligators."

   • Second player: "I am going to Brazil to balance bright blue bananas."

   • Third player: "I am going to Canada to cook colossal cucumbers."

   • Fourth player: "I am going to Detroit to demand delicious dinners."

   • Fifth player: "I am going to Egypt to enchant elegant elephants."

© McGraw-Hill Children's Publishing

0-7424-1940-1 *The Incredible Indoor Games Book*

Yes-No-Black-and-Blue Taboo

Certain words are unavoidable and we say them so frequently that it's difficult to imagine how we would manage without them. Since practice makes perfect, try avoiding the few words in this name game as a beginning.

Materials needed:

None

Room arrangement:

Open space

Time:

15 minutes

Directions:

1. Divide the room in half with an imaginary boundary line. Separate the group into three teams, each team standing in line—one player behind the other—on one side of the boundary line.

2. Explain that you are going to take turns asking players questions and that each player called on must answer immediately—without hesitation. However, players may not use the words *yes, no, black,* or *blue* in their answers or they will lose their turns and go to the end of the line. Players will soon discover that "Maybe" is a good answer and you may have to eliminate that word, too. Players who answer successfully are allowed to cross the boundary line.

3. In order to play fast enough to confuse players, prepare a list of questions beforehand. For example:

   • "Are you eight years old?"

   • "Do you like homework?"

   • "What color is a blue jay?"

   • "Do you have red pajamas?"

   • "Can you ride a bike?"

   • "Do you have twenty toes?"

   • "Is your hair green?"

4. Go from team to team asking questions. As more and more players find ways to answer the questions without using the taboo words, they may join teammates on the other side of the boundary line. The first team to get all its players across the line is the winner.

© McGraw-Hill Children's Publishing 0-7424-1940-1 *The Incredible Indoor Games Book*

Secret Word

In this game players must watch their language. The group tries to trick the player into saying a secret word before that player guesses the word.

Materials needed:

None

Room arrangement:

As is

Time:

15 minutes

Directions:

1. One person, selected to be "It," leaves the room.

2. The rest of the players must agree on a secret word. The word should be a familiar noun or verb used in everyday language, such as *pencil, ruler, map, walk, drink, go,* and so on.

3. After the secret word is selected, the person who is "It" returns to the room. The rest of the players have five minutes to ask the person who is "It" questions, trying to make him or her answer using the secret word. For example, if the secret word is *eraser,* a question might be "How did you correct the mistakes on your homework?" The players should try to make "It" use the word as often as possible within the given time period. One player should keep track of how many times the secret word is used unknowingly.

4. Meanwhile, "It" must try to figure out the secret word from the questions and then avoid saying the word until the end of the time period. A clever player will try to identify obvious pressure from the group to say a particular word. The group must ask general questions that don't give away the word directly.

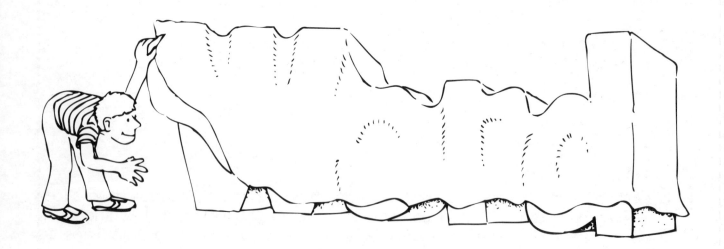

© McGraw-Hill Children's Publishing

0-7424-1940-1 *The Incredible Indoor Games Book*

Name Six

Naming six objects that begin with the same letter is harder than it seems, especially when there is a time limit.

Materials needed:

A key, an eraser, a beanbag, or any other small object

Room arrangement:

Open space

Time:

15 minutes

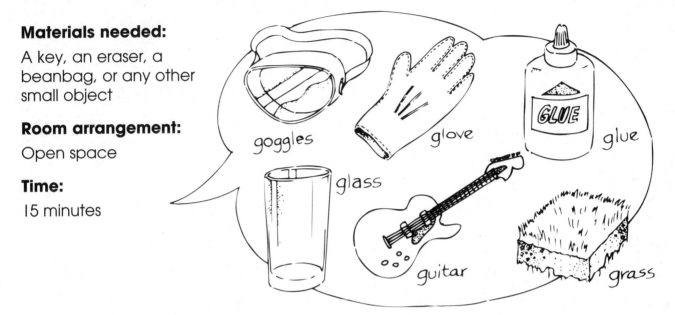

goggles

glove

glue

glass

guitar

grass

Directions:

1. All players sit in a circle. One player stands in the center.

2. The center player closes his or her eyes while the others pass a small object around the circle. When the center player claps hands, the player caught with the object must keep it.

3. The center person opens his or her eyes and gives the person with the object a letter of the alphabet. For fairness, leave out the letter *X*.

4. The player with the object starts passing it around the circle again, meanwhile naming six objects that begin with the letter named. The six objects must be named before the object makes it around the circle.

5. If the player does not succeed in naming six objects by the time the object is passed around, the player must change places with the one in the center. If he or she names six objects successfully, the game continues with the same player in the center.

Variations:

- Younger players can name three or four objects.

- Players name six objects that have a certain characteristic: sticky, blue, hot, or smooth, for instance. The center player may choose the characteristic each player must name.

© McGraw-Hill Children's Publishing 0-7424-1940-1 *The Incredible Indoor Games Book*

Going Blank

Sometimes games can be used to develop our minds in an enjoyable way. Going Blank is a game that people will want to play again and again to test their memories.

Materials needed:

None

Room arrangement:

Open space

Time:

15 minutes

Directions:

1. One person is chosen to be "It." The entire group agrees on three categories. Categories can be anything at all—foods, fruits, cities, shoes, TV stars, singers, flowers, birds, and so forth. For the sake of this example, let's choose shoes, flowers, and birds.

2. The group stands in a circle. The person who is "It" stands in the center, points to anyone in the circle, and names a category: "Shoes!" The person picked must answer within three seconds by naming a kind of shoe: "Loafers!" If the person picked fails to respond, responds incorrectly, or repeats an answer already given, he or she switches places with the one who is "It."

3. The next person who is "It" points to someone across the circle and says "Flowers!" This person responds quickly and says "Daisies!" Next, the person who is "It" might call on the first person again and say "Birds!" This might catch the person so off-guard that he or she cannot even think of a robin.

4. As the game continues, the person who is "It" must keep moving quickly around the circle. One strategy is to hit the same person several times with the same category.

© McGraw-Hill Children's Publishing

0-7424-1940-1 *The Incredible Indoor Games Book*

A What?

When is a key not a key? When it's a bibble! In this game, common objects help create some uncommonly enjoyable confusion.

Materials needed:

2 small common objects (a key, a glove, a pen, or the like)

Room arrangement:

Open space

Time:

15 minutes

Directions:

1. Players sit in a circle on the floor with their legs crossed. The object of the game is to pass two objects around the circle in opposite directions.

2. The leader gives each of the two small objects—perhaps a key and a glove—an imaginary name: "froin" and "bibble." The leader offers one object to the player on the right and says, "This is a froin." The player to whom the object is offered asks "A what?" The leader replies, "A froin," and the object is passed. The leader repeats the same ritual with the "bibble" as he or she hands the object to the player on the left.

3. Both players on the right and on the left continue the ritual, with one exception. When the next player asks, "A what?" the person offering the object turns back to the previous passer and asks "A what?" The "A what?" is passed along back to the leader who tells the name, which is passed back down the line.

4. At some point in the middle, the two objects are going to cross paths. This will appear chaotic, but hang on and keep going.

5. The game ends when both objects find their way back to the leader.

A WHAT?

© McGraw-Hill Children's Publishing 0-7424-1940-1 *The Incredible Indoor Games Book*

As a Rule

Although rules give structure to games we play, most rules are invisible. The following game is all about figuring out the rules.

Materials needed:

None

Room arrangement:

Open space

Time:

15 minutes

Oh, excuse me-- Well, yes-- er-- What was the question again?

Directions:

1. Players sit on the floor in a circle. One person selected to be "It" leaves the room.

2. The players remaining in the room choose a rule to use while answering questions. The rule can be hard or simple, depending on those playing. For example:

   • Answer questions as if you were the person to your right.

   • All boys make up stories and all girls tell the truth (or vice versa).

   • Each answer must begin with the letter of the alphabet following the letter with which the previous answer began.

   • Players must scratch their heads or yawn before answering.

   • Players must answer as if they were their grandparents.

   • Players must answer as if each was an animal.

3. When the person who is "It" comes back, he or she must find out the rule by asking players questions about themselves. The person who is trying to guess the rule is allowed to take as long as he or she needs. If it takes too long, players can help by exaggerating the response the rule calls for.

© McGraw-Hill Children's Publishing 0-7424-1940-1 *The Incredible Indoor Games Book*

Undercover Leader

This popular game challenges the perception of the person who is "It" and requires all players to act carefully so as not to give away a secret leader's identity.

Materials needed:

None

Room arrangement:

Open space

Time:

10 minutes

Directions:

1. Players sit in a circle. One player is chosen to be "It" and is sent from the room. Another player is selected to be the undercover leader. Explain to the group that they must be careful not to blow the leader's cover by looking at him or her directly.

2. The person who is "It" comes back into the room and stands in the center of the circle. The leader begins a movement, such as head nodding, arm moving, or foot tapping, while the rest of the group follows.

3. All those in the circle perform the movements the leader begins. When the leader changes a movement, everyone follows. The person who is "It" must observe very carefully in order to discover the leader.

4. When the leader is discovered, other players are chosen to become "It" and the undercover leader.

49

 0-7424-1940-1 *The Incredible Indoor Games Book*

Objective Evaluation

In this game players put their hands to work as they use their sense of touch to identify a mystery object.

Materials needed:

Small object

Room arrangement:

As is

Time:

15 minutes

Directions:

1. Two players are chosen. One player is called to the front and stands with hands behind his or her back. The other player secretly finds a small object and slips it into the first player's hands.

2. Using the sense of touch, the player tries to identify the object. When the object is identified, the player may look at it.

3. Another player is chosen to be in the front while another searches for a different object.

Quick Change

Memory can be a very selective thing. Often we seem to recall only the things that interest us. This game tests powers of observation and memory. It's fun to see what we miss in front of our very eyes.

Materials needed:

None

Room arrangement:

Open space

Time:

15 minutes

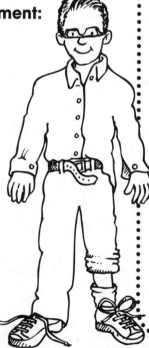

Directions:

1. Each player selects a partner. The partners face each other, observing clothes, hair, accessories, and so on.

2. Next, partners turn their backs on each other and make three changes in their personal appearance, such as unbuttoning a cuff, moving a bracelet, untying a shoe lace, and so on.

3. When both players are ready, they turn around and each tries to identify the changes the other has made.

4. Have players switch partners and make four changes this time. Keep switching partners and adding to the number of changes. Eight changes are usually the most that people can remember.

© McGraw-Hill Children's Publishing 0-7424-1940-1 *The Incredible Indoor Games Book*

Animalisms

A mother hen can tell her chicks' peeping from all the other peeping in the barnyard. Will players be able to identify each other by the sounds of their oinks?

Materials needed:

A blindfold

Room arrangement:

Open space

Time:

15 minutes

Directions:

1. Players stand in a circle. One player, chosen to be "It," is blindfolded and stands in the center.

2. When the person who is "It" says "Go!" the other players begin moving around in a circle.

3. When the person who is "It" says "Stop!" everyone must freeze immediately. The player who is "It" points in any direction. The person pointed to leaves the circle and stands about a foot in front of the person who is "It."

4. The person who is "It" asks the player to make an animal noise—bark like a dog, moo like a cow, meow like a cat, and so forth. The person who is "It" must try to guess the player's identity. If he or she succeeds, the two change places. If the guess is wrong, the person picked returns to the circle and the one who is "It" selects a new player.

© McGraw-Hill Children's Publishing 0-7424-1940-1 *The Incredible Indoor Games Book*

Clapping Clues

With everyone applauding throughout this game, it's difficult to tell who's losing and who's winning.

Materials needed:

Any object

Room arrangement:

As is

Time:

15 minutes

Directions:

1. One person is selected to go out of the room. The rest of the group picks an object for the person to find.

2. The person returns to try to find the object while the group claps. As the person gets closer to the object, the claps become loud and enthusiastic. If the person gets farther away from the object, the claps become quiet and weak.

3. When the object is finally found, the person gets a standing ovation!

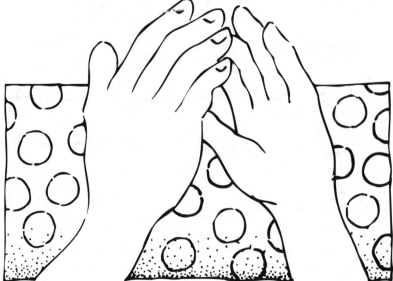

Variation:

Have two people go out of the room while the group members pick a movement or gesture the absent two must do together when they return—shake hands, stick out tongues, hop on one foot, and so on. When the partners return, they must try all kinds of activities in order to find the right one. As the partners get closer to doing the activity—for example, if the activity is to shake hands and they begin to wave their arms—the applause becomes louder until they hit on the right gesture. At that moment, they get a standing ovation as they bow to the audience while performing their gesture.

© McGraw-Hill Children's Publishing 0-7424-1940-1 *The Incredible Indoor Games Book*

Missing Person

How well does each player know the other people in the group? You'd be surprised how hard it is to recall everyone. This game might be subtitled Forget-Me-Not.

Materials needed:

None

Room arrangement:

As is

Time:

15 minutes

Directions:

1. Keep the group seated in one area.

2. One person, selected to be "It," faces away from the group and covers his or her eyes.

3. Another person is selected to leave the room while the rest change their positions.

4. At a signal from you, the person who is "It" turns around and tries to guess who is missing while the group slowly counts to ten.

5. If the person who is "It" identifies the missing person before the group finishes counting, he or she can have another turn. Otherwise, a new person is selected to be "It" for the next game.

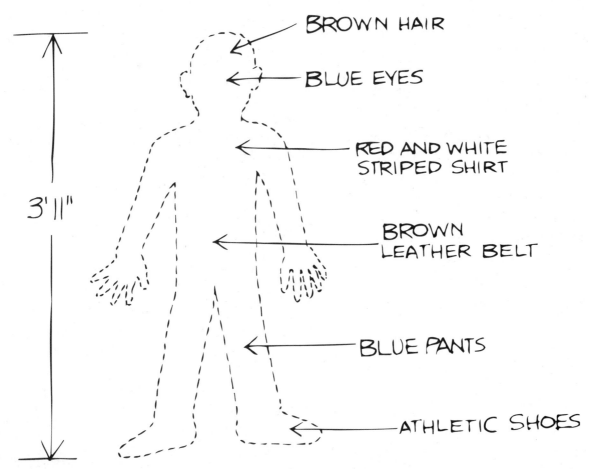

BROWN HAIR

BLUE EYES

RED AND WHITE STRIPED SHIRT

BROWN LEATHER BELT

BLUE PANTS

ATHLETIC SHOES

3'11"

© McGraw-Hill Children's Publishing 0-7424-1940-1 *The Incredible Indoor Games Book*

True Detective

This version of Hide-and-Seek might be called Peek and Seek because players must remain in plain sight without being detected.

Materials needed:

None

Room arrangement:

As is

Time:

15 minutes

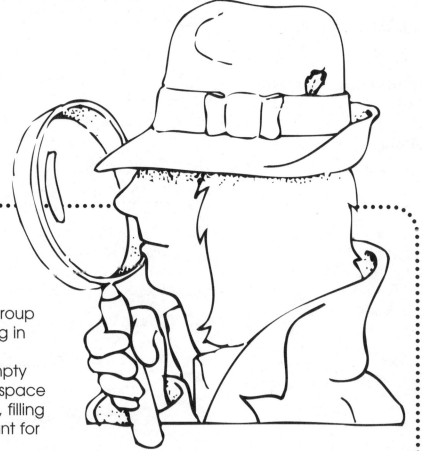

Directions:

1. Before the actual game begins, everyone walks around the room In any direction. To prevent the group from becoming stuck going in only one direction, say, "Whenever you see an empty space, move toward that space and fill it. Then keep going, filling other spaces." It is important for everyone to move silently.

2. After a few moments of walking around, give these instructions: "You are each a detective. Select someone in this room to observe. As you walk around the room make sure you keep that person in sight at all times, but do not let that person know you are watching! Don't be obvious."

3. Let everyone wander around and shadow each other for a few minutes. Remind everyone not to talk.

4. Next, tell players they must try to figure out who is watching them. Have them make it difficult to be seen by dodging in and out of the group. Meanwhile, players have to remember to keep an eye on the person they're observing.

5. To end the activity, say, "Follow your person wherever he or she goes." Players will eventually arrange themselves in a line. Ask players if they properly identified their detectives.

© McGraw-Hill Children's Publishing 0-7424-1940-1 *The Incredible Indoor Games Book*

Basic Elements

Earth, air, fire, and water are the foundations of our environment.
This game helps us appreciate how important the natural elements
are to everyday life.

Materials needed:

None

Room arrangement:

Open space

Time:

15 minutes

Directions:

1. Arrange players in a circle. Select a leader to stand in the middle.

2. The leader points to a player and says one of the elements "Earth," "Air," "Fire," or "Water" followed by "1-2-3."

3. The person pointed to must respond immediately by naming something that depends on that element. For example: If the leader points to a person and says "Air 1-2-3," the player might say "Bird" or "Plane." The same is true for earth and water.

4. If the leader says "Fire 1-2-3," the player must not respond.

5. If a player responds to "fire," hesitates when he or she should answer, or repeats an answer, that player is OUT. The game is played until someone is the winner.

Censored Sevens

Censored Sevens is a counting game, which seems simple enough—except when it comes to sevens. This game is sometimes called Buzz because the word *buzz* replaces all numbers with seven in them and all multiples of seven.

Materials needed:

None

Room arrangement:

As is

Time:

15 minutes

Directions:

1. Players stand in a circle ready to count off. Any time a seven shows up—7, 17, 27, 37, 47, and so forth—and/or a multiple of seven—14, 21, 28, 35, 42, 49, and so forth—the number is replaced by the word *buzz*. For example: 1-2-3-4-5-6-buzz! -8-9-10-11-12-13-buzz!

2. The object of the game is to get to 100 without making a mistake. If one person forgets to buzz, then everyone has to go back to the beginning and start over.

© McGraw-Hill Children's Publishing 0-7424-1940-1 *The Incredible Indoor Games Book*

Number, Please

This game helps to increase players' abilities to concentrate and to listen to clues. It works well as a warm-up activity for group play sessions.

Materials needed:

None

Room arrangement:

Chairs in a circle

Time:

15 minutes

Directions:

1. Players sit in chairs in a circle and count off from one, going clockwise around the room.

2. The game starts when player one calls out the number of another player.

3. The person whose number has been called answers by immediately calling out another number. The next person whose number is called continues by calling another number, and so on. Players are not to hesitate when their turns come. When the game is flowing at its best, the number calling can become fast and furious.

4. Eventually, someone will make a mistake, either by not answering at all, by calling his or her own number, or by calling out a number nobody has. That person moves to the last seat and becomes the largest number in the circle. The rest of the group moves counterclockwise up one seat until the seat of the person who made the mistake is filled. For example, 16 is thinking about the day off next week and doesn't answer when that number is called. So 16 moves to the last seat, which is 30. Then 30 moves to 29, 29 moves to 28, 28 to 27, and so on down the line, until number 17 fills 16's seat. The people whose numbers are below 16 do not move. They stay in their seats and keep their numbers.

© McGraw-Hill Children's Publishing   0-7424-1940-1 *The Incredible Indoor Games Book*

Spellbound

Spellbound is one of those games that could use some magic theatrics, such as a puff of smoke or dramatic gestures. This suspenseful game can be played in a few minutes. The object of the game is to find the person who has the magic touch before you fall under the spell.

Materials needed:

None

Room arrangement:

Open space

Time:

15 minutes

Directions:

1. To begin, the Magician must be chosen secretly so know one knows who it is. To do this, have players stand in a circle with eyes closed. One player, also with eyes closed, stands in the center of the circle and asks all players to hold out their thumbs. The person in the center turns around three times, stopping to pick a thumb. The person whose thumb is chosen is the Magician. Players drop their hands to their sides and open their eyes. Only one knows the identity of the magician!

2. After the Magician is selected, everyone begins to mill around, shaking hands as if it were a fancy party. The Magician turns his or her victims into "stone" with a gentle magical scratch on the palm while innocently shaking hands. When a person feels the magic scratch, he or she does not turn into stone immediately, but continues to move around for a few minutes (so as to not give away the Magician's identity). When the spell does take effect, the player slowly turns to stone with appropriate theatrics (gasping for air, moving like a robot, sinking in slow motion to the floor) and then remains as still as possible until the game is over.

3. Those players not turned to stone must find the Magician by catching him or her giving the magic handshake or by the process of elimination. When a player wants to guess the identity of the Magician, he or she yells, "I reveal!" With hand raised in the air, the player waits for someone to second the revelation. If that doesn't happen, the game continues. If someone does second the revelation, both players stand frozen with hands in the air, count to three, and point together at the suspected Magician. If they point at two different people (even if one is the Magician), the game continues as if nothing had happened. If they point at the same person but that person is not the Magician, they turn to stone. If they pick the Magician, they win! The game ends when the Magician is discovered or when everybody is turned to stone.

© McGraw-Hill Children's Publishing 0-7424-1940-1 *The Incredible Indoor Games Book*

Shapeshifter

This is a lively game played with lots of spirit!

Materials needed:

None

Room arrangement:

Open space

Time:

15 minutes

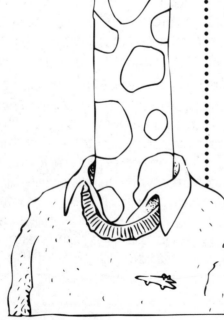

Directions:

1. Players stand in a circle with arms stretched toward the center. Instruct players to close their eyes. Then say "Thumbs up!" Touch one person's thumb and he or she becomes the Shapeshifter. The Shapeshifter can transform people into animals simply by whispering, "You're a cow" (or horse or bird or hippopotamus or whatever). Other players are allowed to speak, but no other player is allowed to say "You're a …" except the Shapeshifter.

2. After the Shapeshifter is selected, everyone begins to mill about as if at a party. Players greet each other, shake hands, and chat.

3. When the Shapeshifter says quietly to another player, "You're a turtle," that player should not give the Shapeshifter away but should, after a few moments, slowly change into the animal. Gradually players will turn into ducks, cows, chickens, and so forth.

4. If a player thinks he or she knows the identity of the Shapeshifter, the player raises a hand and says loudly, "I suspect!" The player then points to the suspect and says, "You're a fish" (or other animal). If the person accused is indeed the Shapeshifter, he or she becomes the animal named. If the accused is not the Shapeshifter, the accuser becomes the animal and the game continues.

© McGraw-Hill Children's Publishing 0-7424-1940-1 *The Incredible Indoor Games Book*

Get It Together

People have countless reasons why they sort and group themselves as they do. In this game, players sort and group themselves and perhaps learn new things about each other in the process.

Materials needed:

None

Room arrangement:

Open space

Time:

20 minutes

Directions:

1. Players line up according to a direction you give. After the direction is given, players must seek information from each other so as to know how to put themselves in order. Here are some examples of the kinds of directions you might give:

   - Line up according to shoe size, from biggest to smallest.

   - Line up according to birthdays, from January to December.

   - Line up in alphabetical order using your last names. Can you rearrange the group to spell a word using the first letter of each last name?

   - Line up according to your home address numbers from lowest to highest.

2. Have everyone gather into groups that have certain characteristics. Here are some examples of characteristics you might name:

   - Gather into groups according to the color of your socks.

   - Gather into groups according to the number of brothers and sisters you have."

   - Gather into groups according to your favorite ice cream flavor.

   - Gather into groups according to your favorite TV star.

© McGraw-Hill Children's Publishing 0-7424-1940-1 *The Incredible Indoor Games Book*

Camouflage

Materials needed:

Small object

Room arrangement:

As is

Time:

10 minutes

Directions:

1. The leader selects a small object, such as a short pencil, nail, penny, paperclip, etc., and shows it to the players.

2. Players leave the room while the leader places the object somewhere in the room where it can be seen without anything being moved. The leader should attempt to find a place in which the object might blend into the background. For example, a penny could be placed on a polka-dot background.

3. The players come back in the room and each one tries to find the object. When a player discovers the object, he or she quietly sits down so as not to reveal the hiding place. If there is one confused player left searching, the group can chime in to help by using the words *hot* and *cold*.

Hmmm...

© McGraw-Hill Children's Publishing

0-7424-1940-1 *The Incredible Indoor Games Book*

Wrong Is Right!

Materials needed:

None

Room arrangement:

Open space

Time:

20 minutes

Directions:

1. Divide players into two groups. Have one player from each group face each other. Have the rest of the players line up in back of them.

2. The object of this game is to be wrong. One of the two players at the head of a line gets to go first and starts by asking the facing player a question like "Are you twenty feet tall?" or "Are there 500 days in a year?" Answers must be immediate. Hesitation puts you out of the game.

3. The person from the other line must answer quickly— but it must be the wrong answer! For example: If the questioner asks "Who was the first president?" and the player responds with "Big Bird," then the player stays. If the player answers "George Washington," then he or she is out of the game and must sit down.

4. The questioner goes to the back of the line. The person who responded "incorrectly" now asks the next player from the opposite team a question.

5. This continues until there is one person left standing or until time is up. The team with the most players left standing when the time is up wins.

© McGraw-Hill Children's Publishing   0-7424-1940-1 *The Incredible Indoor Games Book*

Alien Artifacts

It's been a long journey to this strange planet. Things are very peculiar here. The inhabitants travel on moving pods they call cars and listen to strange noises they call music. They say this place is called Earth! We've discovered some of their artifacts but don't know the purposes the items serve.

Materials needed:

5–10 common objects

Room arrangement:

As is

Time:

20 minutes

Directions:

1. The leader prepares a group of common, manufactured objects and places them on a table in the center of the group. Objects might include a stapler, scissors, crayon, computer disk, piece of yarn, and so on.

2. Players imagine they are aliens from a far-off planet who are seeing these things for the first time. What are they? What are they used for?

3. Give players a slip of paper for each object. Players write their names and the Earth name of the object at the top. Pretending they are alien visitors, they write the new name and use for the object. Encourage players to use their imaginations. For example, a crayon might be a new type of lipstick and a computer disk might be a plate for food.

4. The leader collects all the papers and sorts them into piles by object. Different aliens can be chosen to read the slips of paper. Then the aliens vote for their favorite artifact interpretation.

Variation:

Go around the room and have students give their artifact interpretations orally. The whole class can be given think time before they need to have their ideas ready. Or, this can be a fast-paced game, where students must give immediate, spontaneous answers.

© McGraw-Hill Children's Publishing   0-7424-1940-1 *The Incredible Indoor Games Book*

Ghost Writing

This is a spelling game where finishing a word can have some spooky consequences.

Materials needed:

None

Room arrangement:

As is

Time:

20 minutes

Directions:

1. Determine player order based on seating arrangements (students may sit in a circle, or you can go up and down rows).

2. One player begins by giving the first letter of a word ("p").

3. The next player, thinking of a word that starts with that letter, adds another letter ("p-o").

4. This may bring to mind a word for the third player, who adds another letter ("p-o-r").

5. Now the fourth person adds another letter ("p-o-r-c").

6. The fifth player may finish the word ("p-o-r-c-h"), or may add another letter to keep the word going ("p-o-r-c-u" thinking of "porcupine").

7. A player who ends a word becomes half a ghost. If a player can not figure out how to finish a word (can't think of "pine" to continue "porcu"), he or she may challenge the previous player.

8. During a challenge, the last person to add a letter must explain how the word could have been finished. If the challenged player cannot finish the word (maybe he or she didn't have a word in mind but added a likely letter hoping the next player would think of something) or spells the word wrong, then he or she becomes half a ghost.

9. When a word is finished, the next player begins a new word. As soon as someone becomes half a ghost twice (making them 100% a ghost), he or she is out. The last player "alive" wins the game.

Variations:

- When there are few players, each person can receive one letter in the word *ghost* when he or she ends a word. In this version, a person is not out until he or she has received all letters in the word *ghost*.

- If there are a lot of players or time is limited, players may become full ghosts the first time they end a word.

- For a more lively game, allow the "ghosts" to "haunt" the remaining players. A friendly ghost could whisper a helpful suggestion into a live player's ear. Or, a ghost could pretend to be friendly and whisper a misleading clue. Or, ghosts could just make noises and try to rattle the thinking of the live players.

© McGraw-Hill Children's Publishing 0-7424-1940-1 *The Incredible Indoor Games Book*

Quick! Line Up!

This is a rather active game that needs as much space as possible.
It's not a square dance, but you could call it a dancing square.

Materials needed:

None

Room arrangement:

Open space

Time:

15 minutes

Directions:

1. Arrange the group in a square with an equal number of people on each side. When everyone is in position, stand in the middle.

2. The object of the game is for people on all four sides of the square to remain in the same position in relationship to the person in the middle. This means that people in front stay in front of the leader, people in back stay in back of the leader, people on the right stay on the right, and people on the left stay on the left. When you move to a new position, the people in the square must move themselves to the same relative position as before.

3. To begin, make sure everyone knows his or her position. Then, quickly face in a different direction and say, "Quick! Line up!" Everyone must move as quickly as possible (without running) to reestablish the square around you. You may turn a lot or a little—one time, a 30-degree turn; next time, a quick 360-degree turn into your original position. There are no winners or losers, just the challenge of being a square.

© McGraw-Hill Children's Publishing

0-7424-1940-1 *The Incredible Indoor Games Book*

Person to Person

This game helps bring players closer together in some pretty unusual ways.

Materials needed:

None

Room arrangement:

Open space

Time:

15 minutes

Directions:

1. Each player selects a partner, while one person remains free to be the Caller.

2. The Caller names two body parts that the partners must then try to have touch each other. For example, "Nose to knee" would have one partner bent over with his or her nose touching the other's knee. The contortions can become comically complicated.

3. If the Caller says, "Person to person," everyone must change partners and the Caller selects a partner also. The person left without a partner after the change becomes the new Caller. If some players are inclined to remain Caller for too long, impose a time limit for each Caller.

Kung Thumb

Those in the group who admire martial arts such as karate or aikido can invest this nonviolent wrestling game with all sorts of kung-foolish drama.

Materials needed:

None

Room arrangement:

Open space

Time:

10 minutes

Directions:

1. Everyone picks a partner. Partners stand facing each other.

2. Each player closes one hand into a fist (both partners must use the same hand), raise the thumb, and then opens the fist slightly in order to interlock with the partner's hand. Partners should be clasping hands with thumbs upright.

3. The object of the game is for one partner to put the other's thumb down. As in martial arts meets, all sorts of grunts and shouts add drama to these bouts.

© McGraw-Hill Children's Publishing 0-7424-1940-1 *The Incredible Indoor Games Book*

Nose Toes

Materials needed:
None

Room arrangement:
Open space

Time:
15 minutes

Directions:

1. Have players sit in a circle on the floor.

2. The leader begins by turning to a neighbor and saying "This is my nose," while pointing to his or her toes. The next person repeats, "This is my nose," and points to toes, then adds another silly statement, such as, "This is my ear," while pointing to an elbow. The next person repeats the last sentence—"This is my ear"— and the accompanying gesture, then adds another. This continues around the circle.

3. To keep a lively pace, try having everyone clap in rhythm so that each person will want to move along quickly.

Variation:

Keep everyone clapping in rhythm. One by one, have each player name two body parts while pointing to the opposite. For example, "This is my ear" (while pointing to the nose), "and this is my nose" (while pointing to an ear). After each turn the entire group repeats the statements without missing a beat.

© McGraw-Hill Children's Publishing 0-7424-1940-1 *The Incredible Indoor Games Book*

All Birds Fly

Like Simon Says, this game tries to catch people off guard with the unexpected.

Materials needed:

None

Room arrangement:

Open space

Time:

20 minutes

Directions:

1. One person is chosen to be "It." Standing in front of the group, "It" says, "All birds fly."

2. Next, the one who is "It" names ten things—birds, animals, or objects—and says that they fly. For example, "Eagles fly. Buses fly. Bananas fly. Buildings fly. Robins fly. Rabbits fly. Horses fly. Pigeons fly. Carrots fly. Cookies fly." While reciting the list, "It" flaps his or her arms.

3. Whenever the player who is "It" actually names a bird, all players flap their arms. The object of the game is to catch people flapping their arms when the one who is "It" names something that is not a bird. The player who is "It" can do this by listing things rapidly or staggering things to confuse the group members and catch them unexpectedly.

4. If players flap when something other than a bird is named, they are out of the game. After the person who is "It" finishes listing the ten things, a new "It" is chosen and the players who are out can reenter.

Variation:

This game can be played with other categories, such as "All fish swim" and "All animals walk."

© McGraw-Hill Children's Publishing 0-7424-1940-1 *The Incredible Indoor Games Book*

Balancing Act

This is a tag game in which a player must keep a level head.
If players don't stay cool and calm, they may lose their tops.

Materials needed:

Two clean whiteboard
erasers (or use the box
the eraser comes in)

Room arrangement:

As is

Time:

10 minutes

Directions:

1. Players remain in their seats. One person is chosen to be "It" and is given two whiteboard erasers.

2. The person who is "It" puts one eraser on his or her head and walks around the room. When the person who is "It" puts the second eraser on another player's desk, that player immediately puts the eraser on his or her head and follows the one who is "It."

3. As both players walk, they must balance the erasers on their heads without using their hands. Dropping an eraser means stopping to pick it up and replace it, thus losing time.

4. The second player tries to tag the person who Is "It" before he or she returns to the second player's vacant seat. If the person who is "It" reaches the seat and sits down, the second player receives the other eraser and is the new "It."

© McGraw-Hill Children's Publishing 0-7424-1940-1 *The Incredible Indoor Games Book*

Knot Me!

Are the people in your group fit to be tied? This game will help them unwind.

Materials needed:

None

Room arrangement:

Open space

Time:

10 minutes

Directions:

1. All but two players join hands and form a circle. The two players not in the circle turn away from the circle and close their eyes.

2. The players in the circle twist themselves into a human knot by going over, under, and around arms, legs, and bodies without breaking hands.

3. The two players not in the knot can turn back, open their eyes, and try to figure out how to untangle the group. The group must cooperate with the two untanglers as they try to reverse the twisted knot.

© McGraw-Hill Children's Publishing 0-7424-1940-1 *The Incredible Indoor Games Book*

In Gear

One might call this game a turn on, but it's really an excuse to mesh around.

Materials needed:

None

Room arrangement:

Open space

Time:

10 minutes

Directions:

1. Divide players into groups of 5, 6, 9, and 11 (or comparable numbers).

2. Each group becomes a "gear" by forming a tight circle facing inward and grasping each other's hands.

3. The gears gather in the center of the room. The smallest gear touches the next largest one, which touches the next largest one, and so on.

4. Each player is a "gear tooth." As gears turn, players in one circle are to fit or mesh into spaces between gear teeth in the adjoining circle.

5. The smallest gear begins turning and starts the others turning. The smaller the gear, the faster it turns. The smallest gear can speed up or slow down, causing the other gears to follow suit.

6. You can add to the fun by reversing the direction. Say "Change!" Players make a screeching sound as they put on the brakes and go into reverse.

Human Mixer

Here's a confusing game that sorts itself out in a very entertaining way.

Materials needed:

None

Room arrangement:

Open space

Time:

15 minutes

Directions:

1. Instruct players to stand in a circle. The object of the game is simple: simultaneously, all players must walk directly across the diameter of the circle and reform into a circle. The circle should be exactly the same as before, but with players facing the opposite direction.

2. After players have done this once or twice, have them keep their hands at their sides and not bump into anyone as they walk. Strategies will start to emerge. Some people will walk slowly while others will walk quickly to get across.

3. If a player does accidentally bump into someone else, he or she must say, "Beep!" There will probably be quite a few "beeps" as people cross.

4. Finally, everyone must execute the move across the circle with eyes closed.

© McGraw-Hill Children's Publishing 0-7424-1940-1 *The Incredible Indoor Games Book*

Go!

Bubbling Over

Here's an air-raising experience. Players will float away, but their feet will remain securely on the floor.

Materials needed:

None

Room arrangement:

Open space

Time:

5 minutes

Directions:

1. Push furniture to the edges of the room and divide players into groups of three. "Bubbles" are formed by three players holding hands in a circle.

2. When all the bubbles are ready to take off, they float around the room carefully, not bumping into any other bubbles. Music adds a light touch to this game. Something like a Strauss waltz keeps everyone flying high.

3. Bubbles must try to avoid other bubbles as long as possible. They can spin and twirl gracefully. When bubbles inevitably collide, they pop, then merge into bigger bubbles.

4. As more and more smaller bubbles pop, the large group bubble continues to grow. At the end, the big bubble sadly faces the fate of all bubbles and collapses with a pop on the floor.

Variation:

Try this game with eyes closed.

© McGraw-Hill Children's Publishing

0-7424-1940-1 *The Incredible Indoor Games Book*

Bridging the Gap

There are all sorts of bridges, from simple truss to suspension.
This game adds a new category—the human bridge!

Materials needed:

None

Room arrangement:

Open space

Time:

15 minutes

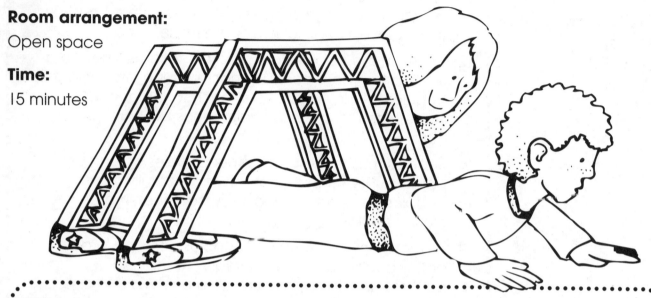

Directions:

1. This is a cooperative activity that involves the entire group. The object of the game is to build a human bridge from one end of the room to the other.

2. Divide the room into two territories with an imaginary valley in between. Explain to the group that everyone must get across the valley in order to escape the terrible ogre who will turn everyone to stone forever! (The story is up to you.) Unfortunately, there is no bridge to get across.

3. After group members are adequately motivated, explain that their only hope is the human bridge! The human bridge is sort of an obstacle course made by everyone in the group. One by one, each person adds to the bridge, standing or crouching in position. Each person must climb over or crawl under the players who are already part of the bridge. For example, the first person might stand with his or her legs apart. The second person crawls under the first person and then crouches into a ball. The third person crawls under the first person and over the second person and ends up as a tunnel on all fours. Players might end up in all sorts of positions, holding arms in hoops for others to step through or lying on the floor for others to step over.

4. This continues as each new player is added. When the last player is added to the bridge, the first player can now crawl through to the other end. This continues until the entire group has moved to the other side of the valley and is safely away from the terrible ogre.

© McGraw-Hill Children's Publishing 0-7424-1940-1 *The Incredible Indoor Games Book*

Chef's Salad

Here's a salad that doesn't need oil and vinegar because
the only things that get tossed around are the players.

Materials needed:

None

Room arrangement:

Chairs in a circle

Time:

15 minutes

Directions:

1. One person is selected to be the Chef. The rest of the group divides into pairs.

2. Each pair chooses a single vegetable. No two pairs should be the same vegetable. If the group is too large, divide vegetables into groups of four.

3. Form a circle of chairs with the person who is the Chef standing in the center. People who are the same vegetable should avoid sitting close together.

4. The Chef calls out a name of a vegetable. Those people whose vegetable is called get up and switch chairs quickly while the Chef tries to grab one of the vacant places. The person who was not able to sit down becomes the new Chef while the former Chef becomes the vegetable.

5. When the Chef calls "Chef's Salad!" everyone changes seats. The player left without a seat is the new Chef.

A safety note: Use sturdy chairs and be sure there is lots of room. If using chairs seems to be too dangerous, have players sit on the floor in a circle.

© McGraw-Hill Children's Publishing   0-7424-1940-1 *The Incredible Indoor Games Book*

Dog Bone

Every dog has its good days and its bad days.
In this game, every dog has a bone to pick.

Materials needed:

A whiteboard eraser, a beanbag, or any other soft object

Room arrangement:

As is

Time:

15 minutes

Directions:

1. Players remain seated except one person selected to be the Dog. The Dog sits with eyes closed, facing away from the group. A "bone"—eraser, beanbag, or other object—is placed behind the Dog and in front of the group.

2. Select one player at a time to try to slip up quietly and get the bone. If the Dog hears a sound, he or she barks like a dog and the would-be bone thief returns to his or her seat. If a player is able to take the bone without being heard, the player returns to his or her seat and hides it. The rest of the group then chants, "Dog, Dog, where's your bone?"

3. The Dog then turns around and has three chances to guess who has the bone. If the Dog guesses incorrectly, the group says "No!" If the guess is correct, the group applauds. In both cases, the one who stole the bone becomes the next Dog.

© McGraw-Hill Children's Publishing

0-7424-1940-1 *The Incredible Indoor Games Book*

Freeze and Thaw

This is not just a cool game. It's freezing cold!

Materials needed:

A bean bag or a clean whiteboard eraser for each player

Lively music

Room arrangement:

Open space

Time:

15 minutes

THIS GAME IS TOO COOL!

Directions:

1. Divide the players into two teams. Each team can select a name such as the Ice Caps or the Glaciers.

2. Give each player a bean bag, whiteboard eraser, or some other small object to balance on his or her head.

3. When the music starts, players walk around the room balancing the objects on their heads. To make it more challenging, have players hop or spin.

4. If an object falls off a player's head, he or she is frozen in place until a fellow teammate—still balancing his or her own object—squats down, picks up the object, and places it back on the frozen teammate's head. Once the object is back on his or her head, the teammate is unfrozen and resumes play. If an object falls off of a rescuing team member's head, then that person is also frozen.

5. The game ends when the music stops. The team that has the most players still active wins.

Variation:

Use a musical chairs style format. Turn the music off at random intervals. Anyone who is frozen when the music turns off is out. Whoever is left unfrozen last is the winner.

© McGraw-Hill Children's Publishing 0-7424-1940-1 *The Incredible Indoor Games Book*

Smaug's Jewels

In J. R. R. Tolkien's book *The Hobbit*, Smaug is a dragon that protects a treasure of gold and jewels. In this game, the dragon may not be as intimidating and the jewels not as priceless, but it is still a challenge to steal the treasure without getting caught.

Materials needed:

A beanbag, a ball of yarn, a handkerchief, or any other small object

Room arrangement:

Open space

Time:

20 minutes

Directions:

1. One person is chosen to be Smaug and stand guard over the jewels (beanbag or whatever). Everyone else forms a circle around Smaug.

2. The group standing around Smaug must try to steal the treasure without being tagged. Those touched by Smaug are frozen in place and can no longer try for the treasure.

3. Smaug must try to defend the treasure. It's always surprising how far loud roars, evil glances, and some fancy footwork will go to ward off invaders. Smaug, if daring, can wander away from the treasure to tag potential thieves.

4. Usually one part of the group will try to tease Smaug away from the loot to help someone from another part of the circle catch the dragon off-guard. The thief can try to dive from behind Smaug and get the jewels before being tagged. If the dragon hovers over the treasure there may have to be a mass charge, which sacrifices a few players for the sake of the jewels.

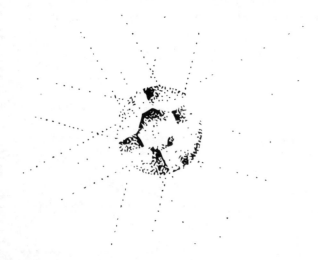

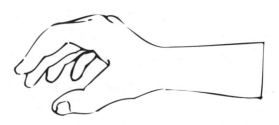

© McGraw-Hill Children's Publishing
0-7424-1940-1 *The Incredible Indoor Games Book*

Traffic Patterns

This game makes rush hour look like a picnic. These rules of the road may drive everyone crazy as players make up their own routes and highways.

Materials needed:

None

Room arrangement:

Open space

Time:

10 minutes

Directions:

1. Players divide into pairs—one is a "car" and the other is the "driver." Cars hold their hands out in front (imitating headlights) and close their eyes. Drivers keep their eyes open and steer cars by standing in back and placing their hands on their partners' shoulders.

2. One set of a car and a driver is chosen to be "It." As in the traditional game of tag, the person who is "It" tries to tag another player. In this game, cars only tag cars. Drivers carefully maneuver cars around other cars, trying to avoid getting tagged. Speeding is not allowed.

3. When the car that is "It" tags another, the car that was tagged becomes the new "It." Cars and drivers switch roles and the game continues.

© McGraw-Hill Children's Publishing

Airport

When large airliners land, they use radar and complicated instruments rather than relying only on the vision of the pilot. In this activity, players rely on senses other than sight.

Materials needed:

Objects found in the room (chairs, books, boxes, shoes, and so forth)

Blindfold

Room arrangement:

Open space

Time:

20 minutes

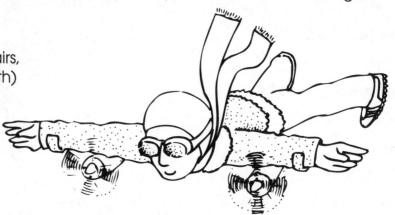

Directions:

1. Divide the group into pairs. One person becomes the "pilot" while the other partner is the "air-traffic controller." One pair runs the course. The rest of the players become the runway by forming two lines about eight feet apart facing each other.

2. Obstacles, such as chairs, books, boxes, shoes, and so on, are placed on the runway. Be careful not to use objects that will be harmful if stepped on or bumped into.

3. The air traffic controller stands at one end of the runway. The pilot is blindfolded and stands at the opposite end. The controller verbally guides the pilot down the runway so that the pilot avoids obstacles and the players on either side.

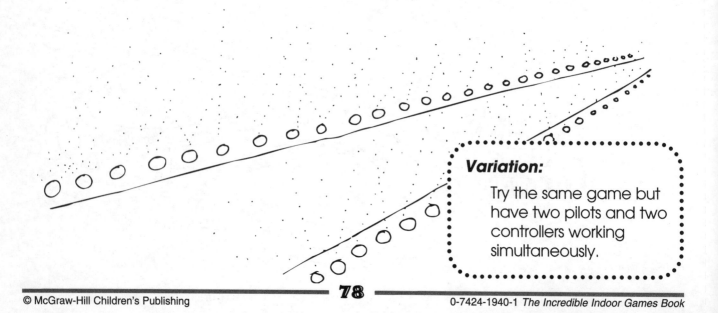

Variation:

Try the same game but have two pilots and two controllers working simultaneously.

© McGraw-Hill Children's Publishing

0-7424-1940-1 *The Incredible Indoor Games Book*

Sticker Stew

This game might be sticker shock for some, but ultimately players will stick together.

Materials needed:

Stickers or adhesive labels

Room arrangement:

Open space

Time:

15 minutes

Directions:

1. Two stickers with the same picture are needed for each player (no two players should have the same stickers). If stickers are not available, give each player two labels with adhesive backing and a marker. Each player writes his or her name or draws a unique design on a pair of labels (each pair needs to look the same, but differ from all the other pairs).

2. Place stickers or labels (with their backings still on!) in a container and mix them up. Each player randomly selects two different labels or stickers that are not his or her own.

3. Players remove the backing and place one sticker on the outside of each shoe. The stickers should be placed so they can easily be seen by other players.

4. Players try to match up shoes with identical stickers. For instance, if one player locates another player with cat stickers on his or her shoes, both players put their feet together, shoe to shoe. These two players must work together to find the matches for their other shoes.

5. Eventually, everyone will be connected together in a tangle of shoes.

Variation:

Place stickers on elbows or hands and have matching players link elbows or hold hands. Or, place stickers on knees.

© McGraw-Hill Children's Publishing 0-7424-1940-1 *The Incredible Indoor Games Book*

Indoor Tag Games

The object of tag is always the same—to flee the deadly touch of the person who is "It" and to remain free. Outdoors, tag is a very active and wide-ranging game. To play it indoors, you must modify the game. The variations here work well in a limited space.

Materials needed:

None

Room arrangement:

Open space

Time:

10 minutes each

Directions:

Ballet Tag

1. It may seem impossible to keep everyone slowed down in the heat of tagging, but if tag were changed into a dance, like a takeoff on a ballet, the game could become more like theater than battle. To get players in the mood, ask them to demonstrate some slow-motion "ballet" movements, such as gracefully twisting bodies, waving arms, and standing on toes.

2. Introduce music; something outrageously Straussian is fun. Keep the movements very slow. Even if the players hate the music, they tend to mock it with exaggerated movements that add to the game.

Popcorn Tag

1. Games work differently with each group. If Ballet Tag isn't active enough and running is too active, try Popcorn Tag. To begin, all players hop up and down on both feet.

2. When the person who is "It" tags a player, the two immediately join hands. The two hopping "Its" set out to tag other helpless hoppers. When other players are tagged, they join the hopping chain until there is only one lonely hopper left.

© McGraw-Hill Children's Publishing 0-7424-1940-1 *The Incredible Indoor Games Book*

Indoor Tag Games (cont.)

Directions: (cont.)

Dog Tag

1. Furniture makes this game more challenging. First, define boundaries—places players cannot go.

2. Everyone gets down on all fours. In this game, players who are tagged are frozen and can't move until other players crawl under them and thaw them out. If the person who is defrosting a frozen player gets tagged in the process, he or she becomes frozen as well. The object of the game is for the one who is "It" to freeze all players.

Alligator Tag

1. In this version of tag the room is transformed into a swamp and the players become reptiles. Have players gather in a circle and lie on their stomachs with faces toward the center. The person chosen to be "It" is in the middle of the circle, also lying on the floor.

2. When "It" says "Go!" the other alligators must scramble away. Remind players to stay on their stomachs. And please, no biting!

Slow Freeze Tag

1. This is less a competitive game of tag and more of a theatrical performance. To begin, divide the group in half—one group to play, the other group to be an audience.

2. Clear as much space in the room as possible, establishing boundaries away from the walls. One person is selected to be "It."

3. Players run in slow motion. When "It" tags another player, the person who is "It" freezes in position and the tagged person becomes the new "It." As more and more people are tagged, the old "Its" remain frozen in whatever position they were in. The last person to remain unfrozen wins.

Variations:

Tag is the perfect game to invent your own variations.

- Have the person who is "It" try tagging while everyone's eyes are closed.

- Have people who are tagged crawl backwards.

- Combine Ballet Tag with Popcorn Tag—players dance until they're tagged, then begin hopping after other players.

© McGraw-Hill Children's Publishing 0-7424-1940-1 *The Incredible Indoor Games Book*

Sit and Run

Materials needed:

2 folding chairs

Room arrangement:

Open space

Time:

20 minutes

Directions:

1. Divide the group into two teams. Players should form two lines at one end of the room.

2. At the opposite end of the room, place two folded chairs on the ground (one chair for each team).

3. At the word "Go!" the first player on each team runs to a chair, opens it, sits down, and counts to ten as quickly as possible. Then he or she folds the chair, places it back on the floor, and runs back to tag the next player.

4. The team that finishes first wins the race.

Variation:

Instead of using folding chairs, have students run past a line marked off on the floor with masking tape. Behind that line, players must sit on the floor and spin themselves around in a circle (while sitting) three times before getting up and running back to tag the next team member.

© McGraw-Hill Children's Publishing 0-7424-1940-1 *The Incredible Indoor Games Book*

Fruit Salad

In this game players become the ingredients in a delicious fruit salad.

Materials needed:

Beach ball, balloon, or sponge ball

Room arrangement:

Open space

Time:

20 minutes

YOU'RE A PEACH!

Directions:

1. Each player selects a name based on a fruit (or vegetable), like Banana, Tangerine, Grape, Pineapple, etc.

2. Six to ten players stand in a circle and pass a balloon, beach ball, or sponge ball back and forth at random.

3. Each time a player passes the ball to another person, he or she calls out his or her own name ("I'm Banana!").

4. After a few rounds of this, the Fruit Salad challenge begins. Now each time a player passes the ball, the player must call out the name of the person to whom he or she is passing ("You're Grapefruit!"). If the player forgets, he or she may ask "What's your name?"

5. As the players become more confident, you may add another ball. This makes the game more exciting. Add as many balls as possible until the players in the Fruit Salad become too mixed up.

© McGraw-Hill Children's Publishing

0-7424-1940-1 *The Incredible Indoor Games Book*

Dot's Dots

If you've ever completed a dot-to-dot drawing, you realize that there is usually only one solution. In this version, absolutely nobody knows what the picture will be! The solution comes from the imagination of the player.

Materials needed:

A sheet of standard-sized blank paper for each player

A pencil for each player

Room arrangement:

As is

Time:

20 minutes

Directions:

1. Give a sheet of paper and a pencil to each player.

2. Have each player cover the surface of the paper with 20 to 30 dots. The dots should be large and easy to see. They should be scattered randomly over the paper.

3. Each player passes his or her paper to a neighbor.

4. Tell players to look hard at the dots to see if they can imagine pictures and then connect the dots so that the picture emerges. This isn't as easy as it seems. Sometimes, turning the paper in different directions is helpful. Encourage far-out solutions to this perplexing problem.

5. After the dots have been connected and the drawings are complete, have each player exhibit his or her drawing.

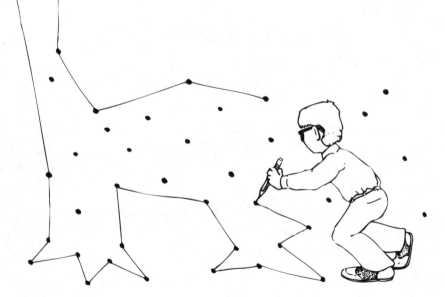

© McGraw-Hill Children's Publishing   0-7424-1940-1 *The Incredible Indoor Games Book*

Scribbles

Our imaginations are always working to organize and structure the world, even if no structure exists. We look up at the clouds and see faces take form in their billowy masses. We look down at a crack in the sidewalk and find the shapes of animals and monsters. This activity is another challenge for our ingenuity.

Materials needed:

A sheet of standard-sized paper for each player

A pencil for each player

Room arrangement:

As is

Time:

20 minutes

Directions:

1. Pass out a sheet of paper and a pencil to each person.

2. The object of this game is to turn the most pointless scribble into something recognizable. Each person draws a simple scribble on the paper and passes it to a neighbor.

3. Now everyone must make this new scribble part of a drawing of a recognizable object or scene.

4. After everyone has finished, have players try to pick out the original scribbles. The one with the most ingeniously disguised scribble gets the Scribble of the Year Award.

© McGraw-Hill Children's Publishing

0-7424-1940-1 *The Incredible Indoor Games Book*

Ripped Puzzles

What a delight! It's okay to tear the paper!

Materials needed:

A sheet of standard-sized paper for each player

A pencil for each player

Room arrangement:

As is

Time:

20–30 minutes

Directions:

1. Hand out a sheet of paper and a pencil to each player.

2. Each person must make a drawing, keeping it hidden from the other players. Have players make their pictures as complicated as they possibly can, with lots of details covering the entire surface.

3. When all are finished drawing, have them tear their pictures into an agreed upon number of pieces; 30 or 40 is plenty. The number depends on the size of the paper, but don't make the pieces unreasonably small.

4. Everyone passes his or her puzzle to another player, who tries to reassemble it. The first player to finish gets a ripping round of applause.

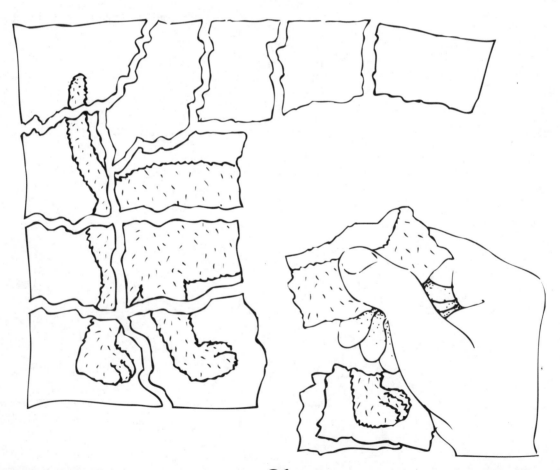

© McGraw-Hill Children's Publishing 0-7424-1940-1 *The Incredible Indoor Games Book*

Mutual Monsters

What would happen if we could switch heads, torsos, and legs with other people? We'd come up with some strange combinations. Prepare yourself, because here we go!

Materials needed:

A sheet of any standard-sized paper for each player

A pencil, crayon, or a felt-tipped marker for each player

Room arrangement:

As is

Time:

20 minutes

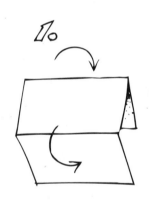

Directions:

1. Give each player a piece of paper and a pencil. Have everyone fold the paper into thirds.

2. On the top third of the paper, each player is to draw the head of a person, an animal, or a made-up creature, continuing the lines on the neck a little bit past the fold. Then, players are to fold back the tops so that the pictures are not visible to anyone.

3. Each person then passes his or her sheet to a neighbor, who is to draw a torso and arms in the middle third without looking at the head drawn on the top third. The lines should again be extended slightly beyond the next fold. Once again, papers are folded so that the pictures cannot be seen and then passed along.

4. The last player connecting the lines adds legs on the bottom third of the paper.

5. When all players have finished drawing, the sheets are unfolded and shown to the whole group.

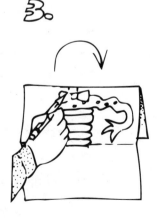
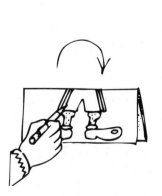

© McGraw-Hill Children's Publishing   0-7424-1940-1 *The Incredible Indoor Games Book*

Graph-Paper Drawings

Grid patterns are the basis of a great many designs—everything from newspaper graphics to skyscraper facades to city blocks to checkerboards. This activity may cover some as yet unknown possibilities.

Materials needed:

A sheet of graph paper for each player (the smaller the squares the better)

A pencil or fine-line, felt-tipped marker for each player

Assorted crayons

Room arrangement:

As is

Time:

20–30 minutes

Directions:

1. Give each player a sheet of graph paper and a pencil or marker.

2. Players should conjure up a mental picture of something very common—a flower, an animal, a building, or a person. Ask players to think about the details of their pictures—the petals of the flower, the tail on the animal, the windows in the building, and so forth.

3. The task is to draw the picture using the lines in the graph paper. Curves will become a series of small, straight, step-like lines.

4. After the outlines are finished, players can color them with crayons and markers to create texture.

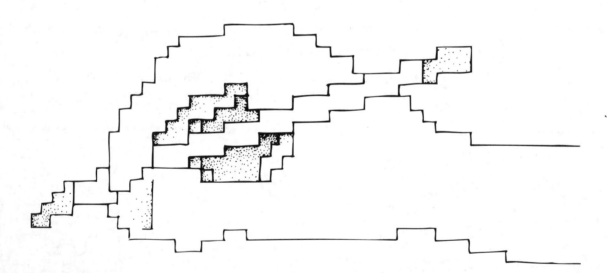

Variation:

Have players think of as many pictures as they can to fill in the small grid squares with tiny drawings.

© McGraw-Hill Children's Publishing

0-7424-1940-1 *The Incredible Indoor Games Book*

Finger Festival

An infant's first toys may be fingers and toes. Why abandon those original playthings? This activity explores some digital delights.

Materials needed:

Watercolors or tempera

A small brush for each player

A cup of water for each group of players

Soap

Towels

Room arrangement:

As is

Time:

25 minutes

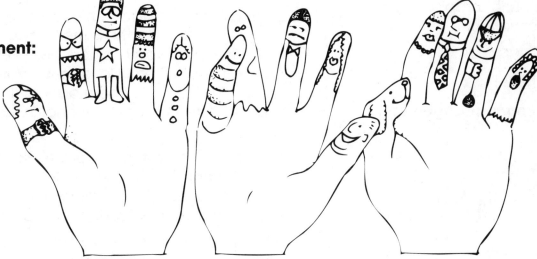

Directions:

1. For this activity arrange players in groups of five or six.

2. Give each group a set a watercolors or tempera and brushes.

3. Have everyone raise the hand he or she does not write with. This is the hand that will have the finger puppets.

4. Each finger has a personality of its own. What kind of character could the thumb be? The index finger? How should each be dressed? Should some wear sunglasses, hats, or neckties?

5. Everyone paints faces and clothes on their fingers. Players can help each other paint.

6. As the final step, organize a Finger Festival with music and dancing fingers. Suggest that players introduce their fingers to each other and choreograph an all-finger production number. Then have players wash their hands.

Tip:

This activity works best when there are parent volunteers or classroom aides to help monitor the mess.

© McGraw-Hill Children's Publishing 0-7424-1940-1 *The Incredible Indoor Games Book*

Give 'Em a Hand

With a little imagination, players can find hidden personalities
in their hands and can use paints to help those special traits emerge.

Materials needed:

Watercolors or tempera

A brush for each player

A cup of water for each
group of players

Fabric scraps or pieces
of yarn or felt

Soap

Towels

Room arrangement:

As is

Time:

30 minutes

Directions:

1. For this activity, arrange players in groups of five or six.

2. Give each group a set of watercolors or tempera and brushes.

3. Each player should raise the hand that he or she does not write with. This is the hand that will be the puppet. Ask players to study their hands to find the personalities in them. Have them move their hands, wiggle fingers, make them dance, float like birds, and make fists to see what characters or creatures start to emerge.

4. Everyone can start to decorate. Players might paint faces on hands, using fingers for arms, legs, strands of hair, or noses. To get more elaborate, they can find small pieces of fabric for collars and hats.

5. Organize three-minute puppet shows with several characters—and don't forget to give them a hand at the end before they wash.

Tip:

This activity works best when there are parent volunteers or classroom aides to help monitor the mess.

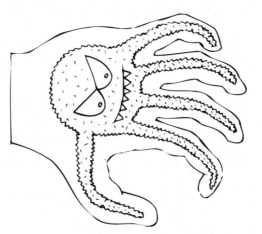

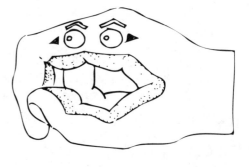

© McGraw-Hill Children's Publishing   0-7424-1940-1 *The Incredible Indoor Games Book*

Fingerprint Pictures

We have discovered the individual personalities of our fingers and uncovered the characters of our hands. So what's left? Maybe the question should be what's left or right? The prints of all ten fingers, of course!

Materials needed:

Inkpads

A sheet of paper for each player

Crayons or fine-line, felt-tipped markers

Soap

Towels

Room arrangement:

As is

Time:

25 minutes

Directions:

1. Divide players into groups of three. Give each person a piece of paper and a crayon or marker. Give each group an inkpad to share.

2. Ink up fingers by pressing tips into the inkpad.

3. Players should gently but firmly press their inked fingers on the paper, adding extra pressure with their other hands. It is helpful to experiment with different printing techniques such as rolling fingertips across the paper.

4. After fingerprints have been printed on the paper, what kinds of things can players make from them? Ask for some suggestions to help get imaginations working.

5. Everyone can complete fingerprint pictures with markers and crayons. Just a few lines will transform these little blotches into wonderful beings. Later, players can try printing the sides and heels of their hands to get more complicated forms.

6. Be careful to remove ink from hands just as soon as the project is finished. Thorough washings with soap and water will be necessary.

Tips:

• This activity works best when there are parent volunteers or classroom aides to help monitor the mess.

• Put cold cream on fingers before inking. This will make cleaning up easier.

© McGraw-Hill Children's Publishing

Big Flip

Everyone will flip over this instant "movie."

Materials needed:

A 3" x 5" file card for each player

A felt-tipped marker for each player

Room arrangement:

As is

Time:

15 minutes

Directions:

1. Give each person a file card and a marker.

2. Everyone should agree on a simple basic shape (a circle, a square, a triangle, and so forth) to draw on the cards.

3. Each player should draw the shape, changing its size or position just a tiny bit. For example, if everyone agrees to draw one circle, some can be as large as the edges of the card, while others can be small and placed in various positions on the cards, while still others could be slightly distorted with little bulges or indentations.

4. Collect the cards and try to arrange them so the shapes seem to progress from card to card.

5. Neatly stack cards in a pile, holding them tightly on one end, and flip! The faster the cards are flipped, the more the shape will appear to dance and wiggle all over.

Little Flipper

Still pictures can move in a flash with this compact movie studio.

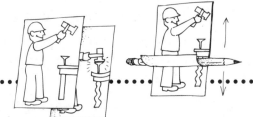

Materials needed:

2 sheets of 3" x 5" paper for each player (transparent enough for tracing)

A pencil for each player

Room arrangement:

As is

Time:

10 minutes

Directions:

1. Pass out two sheets of three- by five-inch paper and a pencil to each player.

2. Players should think of a repetitive movement, such as a carpenter hammering a nail, two people shaking hands, or someone waving goodbye.

3. Players draw one picture depicting that movement on one of the two sheets. Then, on the other sheet of paper, they trace the first picture, but slightly change the position of the head, arms, or feet.

4. Next, players take one of the sheets and roll it around the pencil so that it curls. Place the curled picture on top of the flat one. Move the pencil back and forth rapidly to flip the picture and watch it move.

© McGraw-Hill Children's Publishing   0-7424-1940-1 *The Incredible Indoor Games Book*

Paper Ornaments

The most versatile material readily available is paper. A sheet of paper is flexible; yet when folded properly, it can support a brick. In this activity, students explore paper possibilities and at the same time decorate the classroom.

Materials needed:

200 to 300 sheets of paper (construction paper, recycled paper, and so forth)

Scissors for each player

Hole punchers

Staplers

Medium-weight string

Crayons and felt-tipped markers (optional, for additional decoration)

Room arrangement:

As is

Time:

35–45 minutes

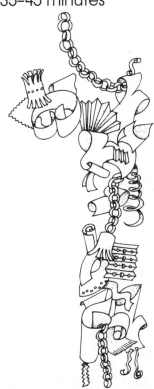

Directions:

1. Divide the players into groups of four or five. Give each group a stack of paper, scissors, a stapler, and a hole punch.

2. There are many different techniques for making paper ornaments, but for this activity encourage players to experiment with inventing their own shapes. To help players get started, demonstrate some of the basic things that can be done with paper. For example:

   • rolling—curling into a cylinder
   • twisting—bending into a form
   • pleating—folding into a repeated pattern
   • folding—randomly creasing into free forms
   • cutting—slicing into shapes and fringes
   • crumpling—crushing and flattening into a textured surface
   • tearing—ripping into natural forms
   • scoring—pressing a line into the surface to make clean folds
   • punching—poking out surface designs and textures

3. Each player takes several pieces of paper and begins to experiment using one or more of these techniques. Paper designs do not have to represent anything. Allow players to cut, twist, and punch their way to creativity. For an added challenge, see who can cut the longest continuous ribbon from a single sheet of paper, punch the most holes to make a lacy design, or create the largest paper decoration.

4. Tie a piece of string across the room for a paper-ornament display. How many paper ornaments would it take to cover the entire ceiling? Paper ornaments can be used in conjunction with other activities such as paper costumes and puppets.

© McGraw-Hill Children's Publishing

Body Coverings

Making costumes can be done quickly with this basic body covering.
Additions can be added instantly, making the costume any creature imaginable.

Materials needed:

Roll of brown paper 36" wide

Scissors for each player

Tape

Staplers

Crayons or felt-tipped markers

Room arrangement:

Open space

Time:

40 minutes

STAPLE EDGES

ADD PAPER DECORATIONS

Directions:

1. Roll out brown paper across the floor. Cut a strip four or five feet long for each person.

2. Have everyone fold his or her strip in half. Folded strips can be cut into various shapes:

   • Cut a half circle from the folded edge to make a poncho-type covering.

   • Cut the edges of the paper into a shape that fits around head and arms.

   • Cut out a space for the face and cut a whimsical design around the edges.

   • Create a blob shape or cut a fringe along the bottom.

3. Staple edges around the head and arms, leaving enough extra room for movement.

4. Add paper decorations with tape or stapler. Draw designs directly on the costume with crayons or felt-tipped markers.

5. Although it's not absolutely necessary, it's a good idea to have a mirror so that players can see themselves transformed. Organize a costume fashion show and have players parade through the room. Add a little music and clapping in rhythm and you have the makings of an old-time jig.

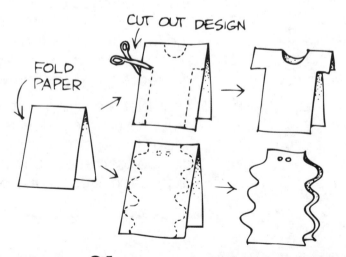

CUT OUT DESIGN

FOLD PAPER

94

© McGraw-Hill Children's Publishing

Nose Masks

Masks provide instant identities and, in this case, instant expressions.
The eyes don't have it, the nose do—er, does.

Materials needed:

A sheet of 5 1/2" x 8 1/2" paper for each player (cut pieces of 8 1/2" x 11" paper in half)

Crayons or felt-tipped markers

Scissors

Room arrangement:

As is

Time:

20 minutes

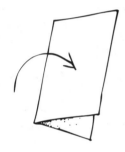

FOLD

Directions:

1. Give each player a piece of paper and a crayon or marker.

2. Players fold their sheets of paper in half and cut a hole for the nose from the folded edge. Since noses are smaller than one might think, start by having everyone cut a small triangular shape from the folded edge. When unfolded, it becomes twice as large so it is better to start small and trim away later.

3. After nose holes have been adjusted, have players put the papers on their noses. When all masks are securely fixed, tell everyone to search for their eyes and carefully mark eye locations with a crayon. Next, take off the masks and poke a tiny hole for each eye.

4. Decorate masks with faces and expressions. Draw a mouth and two eyes (or three eyes, for that matter). Suggest some characteristics—a grouchy frown, a wink, a smile, or even an imaginary face.

5. After masks are finished, everyone can put on an instant expression—ready to face the next assignment.

CUT HOLE
FOR NOSE

UNFOLD AND
DRAW A FACE

PLACE
ON
NOSE

© McGraw-Hill Children's Publishing

Intergalactic Paper-Bag Masks

Every child who has grown up in this world of supermarkets has probably made a mask from a grocery bag. Now this simple activity can turn an everyday brown bag into the stuff of science fiction.

Materials needed:

A brown paper grocery bag for each player

Scissors

Assorted-color felt-tipped markers

Masking tape

White glue

Paper scraps, aluminum foil, and other leftover materials

PUNCH OUT EYE HOLES

ADD PAPER SHAPES AND FOIL

Room arrangement:

As is

Time:

40 minutes

TRIM TO REST ON SHOULDERS

Directions:

1. Give each player a grocery bag. Players can share scissors, felt-tipped markers, tape, glue, and scrap materials.

2. Introduce this activity as something out of this world. Tell players that masks should represent beings from another world or galaxy. Each player must make up his or her own creature, give it a name (Venox, Zipnoid, whatever), and try to imagine its biography—where it lives, what it does for a living, what it eats, and so forth.

3. To construct masks, have players put bags over their heads and find eye positions. You may have to trim the bottom of the bag so it rests comfortably on small shoulders. Mark eye locations with felt-tipped markers. Remove bags and punch eyeholes with the scissors.

4. To decorate masks, players can cut pieces of paper and foil to create fantasy eyes, noses, and ears. Paper can be fringed, torn, twisted, and folded into shapes that can be applied to the surface of the bag.

5. When masks are completed, organize an intergalactic convention of spaced-out creatures to meet, exchange names, and share cultural differences.

© McGraw-Hill Children's Publishing 0-7424-1940-1 *The Incredible Indoor Games Book*

Invasion of the Paper-Bag Puppets

Materials needed:

A paper bag for each player (lunch-bag size)

Assorted-color paper

Paper plates

Yarn, buttons, fabric scraps, foil, and other leftover materials

Scissors

Masking tape or cellophane tape

White glue

Room arrangement:

As is

Time:

30 minutes

Directions:

1. Players can share materials. Pass out a paper bag to each person and distribute scissors, glue, tape, and decorative supplies.

2. Before players begin to decorate puppets, talk with everyone about an imaginary land from which all the puppets come. What kind of place is it? Do inhabitants live in the same manner as we do?

3. What do they wear? What do they look like? What do they sound like? After some discussion about these puppet creatures, everyone can begin to make his or her own creature.

4. Encourage players to cut and paste paper and scraps rather than just draw with felt-tipped markers. Hair can be fringed paper, tongues can be cut fabric, and tails can be braided yarn. Fold a paper plate in half and attach it for an instant mouth, or use paper plates for ears and arms.

5. As more and more puppets from the imaginary land begin to invade the classroom, they will probably begin to explore their newfound landscape. Students may interact with puppet gibberish or you may want to teach them a few games that are played in the imaginary world. Try sitting in a circle and letting the puppets play some games!

© McGraw-Hill Children's Publishing

Newspaper Headgear

Some people wear hats to cover their heads and some people wear hats to express themselves. Newspaper hats are not much protection against rain, sleet, or falling space junk, but they offer plenty of opportunity for some headstrong self-expression.

Materials needed:

Newspapers

Masking tape

Scissors

Staplers

Room arrangement:

Open space

Time:

25 minutes

Directions:

1. Push desks and chairs to the edges of the room and stack newspapers, tape, scissors, and staplers in the center. Players can work on the floor. Keep a wastepaper basket close by for cleanup.

2. Before everyone begins, talk with the group about hats. Make a list of the varieties, such as chefs' hats, pirate hats, space helmets, feather headdresses, crowns, and so on.

3. Have each player take a sheet of newspaper and invent his or her own hat. Newspaper can be twisted into cones, cut into fringes, folded into caps, and made into any shape. Since newspaper is plentiful, allow players to use as much paper as they need.

4. When players are finished and the activity has gone to their heads, a hat parade with music is in order.

© McGraw-Hill Children's Publishing 0-7424-1940-1 *The Incredible Indoor Games Book*

Newspaper Dowels

Old news is good news to newspaper recyclers. Newspaper can become a great building material that may make tomorrow's headlines.

Materials needed:

Newspapers

Masking tape

Room arrangement:

Open space

Time:

35–45 minutes

Directions:

1. Move furniture to the edges of the room and place a stack of newspapers in the middle. Demonstrate how to roll a single sheet of newspaper tightly into a dowel. Begin at one corner and roll diagonally, making it as hard and as inflexible as possible. Fasten with masking tape.

2. Join newspaper dowels together at ends with masking tape.

3. Players can build paper dowel structures on the floor. (Three dowels taped into a triangle are the strongest building unit, but allow players to experiment with different shapes.) Each player can construct his or her own structure, or everyone can work together on one gigantic construction that will fill the whole room. For added decoration, fill in the framework with panels of colorful paper and drawings.

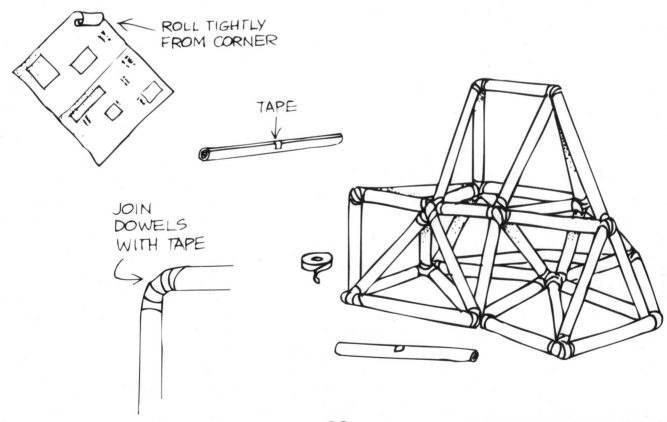

ROLL TIGHTLY FROM CORNER

TAPE

JOIN DOWELS WITH TAPE

© McGraw-Hill Children's Publishing

Fast Forests

This project will transform any room into a forest in minutes. It's an activity that can create a backdrop for an instant play or just a change of atmosphere.

Materials needed:

4 to 6 full-sized, double-spread sheets of newspaper for each player

Scissors

Masking tape

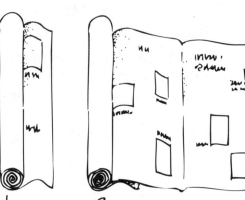

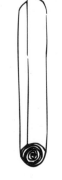

Room arrangement:

Open space

Time:

25 minutes

Directions:

1. Give each player four to six sheets of newspaper. It is helpful if you demonstrate each step.

2. Roll a sheet up from a narrow end, leaving about two inches unrolled. Slip another sheet into the extended, unrolled piece and continue rolling. Do the same with a third and fourth sheet. The more newspapers sheets that are added, the larger the tree will be, but it becomes more difficult to cut. When the last piece of paper has been added, roll firmly. Fasten with masking tape, on what will be the bottom end of the roll.

3. Flatten one end of the roll and, using sharp scissors, cut halfway down the length of it.

4. Now flatten the same end so that the cuts are on the sides. Cut again in the center so that the end is now cut into quarters.

5. Hold the newspaper roll at the uncut end and shake, loosening the newspaper "leaves." Finding the center of the leaves, pull gently and watch the tree grow. To display trees in the room, tie a string across the room from wall to wall. Attach string to treetops and hang in a row.

© McGraw-Hill Children's Publishing 0-7424-1940-1 *The Incredible Indoor Games Book*

Gliders

Although paper airplanes have been around for decades, this version is relatively new and has found much popularity among paper pilots.

Materials needed:

A plastic drinking straw for each player

2 paper clips for each player

A sheet of 4 1/4" x 11" construction paper for each player (8 1/2" x 11" paper divided in half)

A pencil for each player

Rulers

Scissors

Room arrangement:

As is

Time:

20 minutes

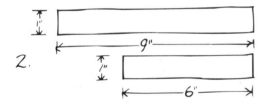

Directions:

1. Players may work at tables or desks. Give each player a drinking straw, a piece of paper, two paper clips, and a pencil. Have enough rulers and scissors on hand to share.

2. Each player cuts out two strips of paper, one strip 1" by 9" and the other 1" by 6". Players should write their names on one of the two strips to avoid any mix-ups later.

3. Slip a paper clip into each end of the straw. Make sure that the smaller wire loop is on the inside and the larger loop is on the outside.

4. Roll each strip of paper into a loop and clip one to each end of the straw, making sure that the paper loops are aligned.

5. When everyone is finished, it is time for a test flight. The suggested glider launch position is to hold the glider in the center with the small loop in front. Don't throw the glider, but gently push it forward so that it will sail. Adjustments can be made to the size of the larger loop to help give the smoothest flight possible.

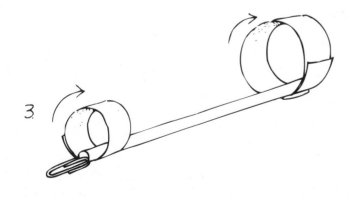

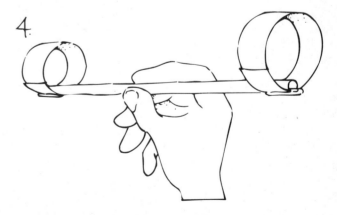

© McGraw-Hill Children's Publishing

0-7424-1940-1 *The Incredible Indoor Games Book*

Wild Blue Yonder

The classic paper plane has been the same since the 1920's. Nearly every child has made dozens, if not hundreds, of paper airplanes, but how many have thought of designing their own? In this activity players test their aeronautical engineering skills.

Materials needed:

As much paper as possible (at least 2 sheets of 8 1/2" x 11" paper for each player)

Scissors

Felt-tipped markers and crayons for additional decorating

Room arrangement:

Open space

Time:

30–40 minutes

Directions:

1. Give each player a sheet of paper. The object of this activity is to invent a new version of the classic paper plane. Players should try flying their unfolded paper to see how even a simple sheet of paper can float and stay aloft.

2. Next, have players fold the paper in half to see what effects that has on its flight. Suggest that players try cutting their paper into the form of a plane, folding wings and edges for reinforcement.

3. After players have explored the qualities of the paper and how it flies, give them another sheet of paper to make final paper planes.

© McGraw-Hill Children's Publishing   0-7424-1940-1 *The Incredible Indoor Games Book*

Wild Blue Yonder (cont.)

Directions (cont.):

Directions (cont.):

Part Two: Fly-Offs

1. After pilots have tested and modified their creations, it's time for the Paper Plane Fly-Offs. Clear the room as much as possible. Move chairs and tables to make a launching area for planes. Those not flying planes should sit at the side as spectators.

2. Judging paper planes can be fun if it is done in a playfully serious manner. Here are several categories:

   • *Duration Aloft.* Since few people carry a stopwatch and watching the second hand on a room clock is almost impossible, it is advisable to have all competitors line up and throw their entries at the same time. The last plane to land is the winner. Two out of three tries might be fairest for everyone.

   • *Distance Flown.* This is easier to judge. Players can fly planes one at a time, leaving them where they land. If there is a tie and both pilots hit the farthest wall, both will have to go again.

   • *Aerobatics and Maneuverability.* Hang a large hoop or box from the ceiling and see who can go through it or hit it. Create an obstacle course with a line of people. See how far planes can go under people's legs. Give pilots an opportunity to show off fancy flying tricks such as a loop-the-loop.

   • *Most Inventive Design.* Although some may not fly well, they still may be great to look at. Have everyone vote for his or her favorite plane design.

© McGraw-Hill Children's Publishing   0-7424-1940-1 *The Incredible Indoor Games Book*

Copters

Not all paper aircraft fly across the room from wall to wall. Some fly vertically. This aircraft may not be big on distance, but it is definitely fun to watch.

Materials needed:

A sheet of 8 1/2" x 11" paper for each player

A pencil for each player

Rulers

Scissors

Room arrangement:

As is

Time:

15 minutes

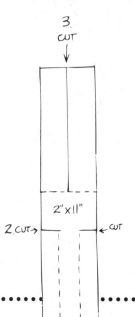

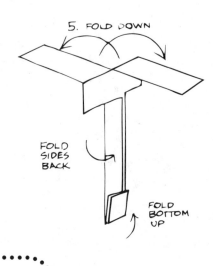

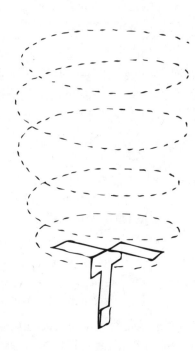

Directions:

1. Give each player a sheet of paper, a pencil, a ruler, and scissors. (Rulers and scissors can be shared if there are not enough for everyone.) You should demonstrate construction while giving instructions.

2. First, have each player measure and cut a 2" x 11" strip of paper. Halfway down the strip, cut two 1/2" slits in each side.

3. Next, cut a slit down 4 inches from the top.

4. Fold the bottom stem to weight it.

5. Fold the top pieces in opposite directions for rotors.

6. After copters are completed, have players hold them upright and drop them from a high place. Organize a mass launch by having players line up in two lines facing each other. On the count of three, have players drop the copters in a huge flurry of spinning paper.

© McGraw-Hill Children's Publishing

0-7424-1940-1 *The Incredible Indoor Games Book*

Things Are Pickin' Up

After a creative activity there are usually paper scraps, scissors, tape, and other materials all over the floor. Cleanup usually isn't fun—unless it becomes a game. Here's a housekeeping game kids are sure to pick up on.

Materials needed:

Leftover scraps on the floor

2 brooms

2 trash bags

2 dust pans

Room arrangement:

A mess

Time:

5 minutes

Directions:

Method 1: Divide and Conquer

1. Divide the group into two teams and the room into two sections. Each team is given a trash bag, a broom, a dustpan, and any other necessary cleaning equipment.

2. The two teams line up in the center, face-to-face. When you say "Go!" both teams race to clean up their area and reassemble back in the center of the room.

3. The first team finished is the winner, but the title is not final until each team inspects the other team's section. If both teams turn up overlooked scraps on the other's side, the game will have to be called a draw.

Method 2: Clean Sweep

1. The entire group lines up together in a cooperative team effort to beat the clock and be the fastest cleaners in the world!

2. Armed with brooms, trash bags, and dustpans, the group stands at attention as you eye the minute hand of the clock. When you say "Go!" the group scrambles to clean every square inch of the room—picking up papers, straightening furniture, and putting equipment back in place.

3. When the room is clean, record the amount of time the cleanup took—which will have to be beaten the next time the room is a mess.

© McGraw-Hill Children's Publishing 0-7424-1940-1 *The Incredible Indoor Games Book*

Is It a Llama?

Materials needed:

Pencils

Crayons

Paper

Room arrangement:

As is

Time:

20 minutes

Directions:

1. Give each player a letter-sized sheet of paper and a pencil.

2. Each person secretly writes the name of an animal on her or his paper and quickly turns it over.

3. Collect the papers and scramble them in a "hat."

4. Each player chooses one sheet from the hat, hiding the name of the animal.

5. At the count of three, players silently read the name of the animal, turn the paper over, and then draw the animal on the back.

6. Number each drawing, starting with 1, and collect them.

7. Lay all the sheets on the floor, drawing-side up.

8. On another piece of paper, have each player write the numbers of all the drawings and the animal each pictures.

9. The player(s) with the most correct answers win(s).

© McGraw-Hill Children's Publishing 0-7424-1940-1 *The Incredible Indoor Games Book*

Air Writing

A great photograph exists of Pablo Picasso drawing in the air with a flashlight. Everyone has probably tried to communicate at some time by spelling out a word or drawing a picture by simply tracing it in the air. This activity was inspired by that idea.

Materials needed:

A list of simple-shaped objects

Room arrangement:

As is

Time:

15 minutes

Directions:

1. Prepare a list of simple objects. Put the name of each object on its own index card.

2. Divide the players into two teams.

3. One member of each team is chosen to go first. The players are shown the object name on the card simultaneously. For nonreaders, the leader may whisper the name of the object.

4. The players return to their respective teams and try to communicate the word by drawing it in midair. The first team to identify the word wins a point.

5. The game continues until each team member has had a chance to draw in midair. The team with the most points at the end of the game wins.

© McGraw-Hill Children's Publishing 0-7424-1940-1 *The Incredible Indoor Games Book*

Encoded E-mails

Our secret agents are receiving very strange e-mails! They are just a jumble of random letters that need to be decoded. For months agents have tried to understand these strange messages. In this game, players are the secret agents trying to crack the code.

Materials needed:

Whiteboard or large sheet of paper

Marker

A sheet of standard-sized paper for each player

A pencil for each player

Room arrangement:

As is

Time:

20–30 minutes

Directions:

1. Give paper and pencil to each "secret agent."

2. Each player says the first letter that comes to mind. As players recite random letters, write them in order of recitation on the board for everyone to see.

3. Each player must silently decode the letters written on the board, writing each letter as the beginning of a new word. For example, the letters L T U V M K F E might be decoded as "Large tomatoes under van. Make ketchup for everyone" or "Like torn umbrellas very much. Keeping for elephants" Players should try to compose messages that make some kind of sense—no matter how silly.

4. Decoded messages should be folded and passed to other players. The secret agents may want to read some of the messages aloud.

Variation:

If players have access to computers and e-mail, select e-mail partners. Have each player send a secret code (random letters) to his or her partner. Then the partner e-mails a decoded response back. Players can share their codes and responses with the class.

© McGraw-Hill Children's Publishing 0-7424-1940-1 *The Incredible Indoor Games Book*

Pots and Pans

No, this game is not about kitchen utensils; it's about things that go together in pairs.

Materials needed:

A sheet of paper for each player

A safety pin for each player

A pencil

Room arrangement:

Open space

Time:

20 minutes

Directions:

1. To prepare, make a list of pairs of things. For example:

   - ham and eggs
   - pepper and salt
   - shoes and socks
   - bread and butter
   - nickel and dime
   - thunder and lightning
   - Romeo and Juliet
   - Tom Sawyer and Huck Finn
   - Jack and Jill
   - twist and shout
   - birds and bees
   - sticks and stones
   - hook and ladder
   - cops and robbers

2. Write the name of one member of each pair on its own sheet of paper.

3. Gather players in a circle with their backs toward the center. Pin a sheet of paper to each back so that the person pinned does not know the word on his or her back.

4. After all players are pinned, each must try to find the person with the mate to his or her word. This is difficult because no player knows his or her own word and is not allowed to ask its identity directly. Players may ask each other any question that can be answered with a yes or a no (Is it a person? Is it an animal?). Players must first identify their own words and then find their partners.

5. The game ends when each player has successfully found his or her partner.

© McGraw-Hill Children's Publishing 0-7424-1940-1 *The Incredible Indoor Games Book*

Name-O-Grams

What's in a name? Lots of letters! Rearrange them and see if they still match their owners.

Materials needed:

A 3" x 5" file card for each player

A pencil for each player

Room arrangement:

As is

Time:

15 minutes

Directions:

1. Give each player a file card and a pencil.

2. Players print their names in reverse; for example, *Jane Jones* would become *Enaj Senoj*.

3. The leader collects the cards, shuffles them, and distributes them to the players.

4. One by one players read aloud the backward names they have received. The rest of the group must try to guess within ten seconds whose name it is.

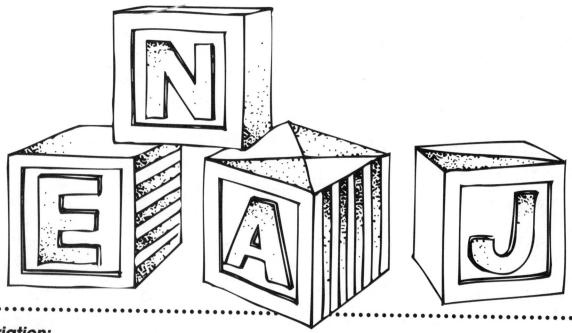

Variation:

1. Players print their names in scrambled order, mixing up letters to spell other words if possible. For example, *Thomas* might become *Hot Sam*.

2. Players fold cards and keep passing them until you say to stop.

3. Players unfold the cards and begin to unscramble the names. When a player unscrambles a name, he or she searches for the player whose name it is. These players join hands. As more and more players' names are unscrambled, pairs become lines, lines join together, and soon there is one large, unscrambled circle.

© McGraw-Hill Children's Publishing 0-7424-1940-1 *The Incredible Indoor Games Book*

Meanwhile, Back at the Ranch

In many movies, two or three stories happen at the same time. Scenes are intercut to show various stories developing. While Groucho is off turning a swanky dinner party into a food fight, his brother Harpo is calmly playing his harp in the swimming pool.

Materials needed:

A sheet of standard-sized paper for each player

A pencil for each player

Room arrangement:

As is

Time:

15 minutes

Directions:

1. The entire group is seated at desks or tables. Each player is given a sheet of paper that is divided into three columns. The group agrees on three different subjects. For example; fruit, foreign countries, and animals might be chosen.

2. When you call out a column number, each player starts to write about the subject in that column. When you call another number, players stop in midsentence and begin to write about the subject in that column. Call out numbers randomly and rapidly: "One!" "Three!" "Two" "Three!" "One!"

3. When sheets are nearly filled, call out "The end!" At this point, players must try to connect all three stories and create some sort of finish. For example, "And so the baby grapefruit left home to see the world only to fall in love with the lonely walrus. They were married under the Eiffel Tower and lived happily ever after in Paris." Players who feel they have a funny or interesting story may want to read it to the group.

© McGraw-Hill Children's Publishing

0-7424-1940-1 *The Incredible Indoor Games Book*

One and Only

Each of us is unique, but in what ways do we show it? Here's a chance for players to reveal what sets them apart from everyone else.

Materials needed:

A 3" x 5" file card for each person

A pencil for each player

Room arrangement:

Open space

Time:

20 minutes

Directions:

1. Give players file cards and pencils and ask them to write descriptions of themselves. The descriptions must point out their unique qualities, experiences, or accomplishments—the things that make them unlike any other person in the group. It's better to describe personality than physical appearance. Players should not sign their names.

2. Collect file cards and shuffle them. Players form a circle and sit on the floor. File cards are passed out. If a player receives his or her own card, players close their eyes and switch cards.

3. One by one, players read the cards they are holding. After each reading, the group tries to guess who wrote it. The goal is to try to guess the identity of the unique person as quickly as possible.

New and Improved

After a while, a product becomes old-fashioned and out of date. It's time to try to repackage the product and attract a new audience. This game reflects the real-life game of advertising.

Materials needed:

10 brand-name products

Pencils

Paper

Room arrangement:

As is

Time:

15 minutes

Directions:

1. The leader selects ten well-known commercial products. Place the objects on a table in the center of the room.

2. Explain to players that each company wants to double its sales and needs a new name for its product to attract interest. Players work for the advertising company, which is trying to get a multimillion dollar contract.

3. Players are given paper and pencils and have 10 to 15 minutes to dream up some catchy new names for these products. (For example, a tissue brand might be Nose Clouds and invisible tape might be Quick Stick.)

4. Players present their new product names to the group one product at a time. Players vote on the best new name for each product. The player whose names get the most votes gets to be the advertising director.

A Long Story

This experiment in cooperative storytelling may not only become the world's longest story, but also the tallest one!

Materials needed:

A roll of business-machine paper
(used with adding machines, cash registers, and so on)

A pencil for each player

Room arrangement:

Open space

Time:

15–25 minutes

Directions:

1. Arrange players in a single line, side by side, and have them sit on the floor. Give each player a pencil. Roll out a ribbon of white business machine paper across the floor in front of the players.

2. Each player is limited to adding three words in each turn to the story line. One by one, players add their words, connecting them to the words of the last player. Players can read the last few words before making an addition, but they should not worry about making perfect sense.

3. After a player adds three words, he or she can go to the end of the line for another turn. It's up to you how long the story gets to be and how many turns the group should have.

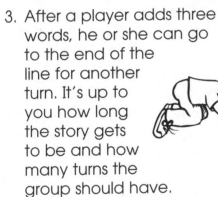

4. The last player to add something can add the last few words to finish the sentence.
For or five readers should take turns reading the story aloud to the group.

© McGraw-Hill Children's Publishing 0-7424-1940-1 *The Incredible Indoor Games Book*

Hidden Treasures

To this day, the lure of hidden treasure prompts people to explore the depths of the oceans and the jungles of uncharted lands. This activity is designed to turn an everyday room into a treasure chest.

Materials needed:

2 sheets of scrap paper
for each player

A pencil for each player

Room arrangement:

As is

Time:

40 minutes

Directions:

1. Pass two sheets of paper and a pencil to each player.

2. Tell each player to draw a treasure secretly without letting anyone else see. It could be something very special, maybe even something not even invented yet—like a round-trip ticket to Mars. Or it could be something that everyone dreams about—a castle in the mountains, a supersonic racecar, or a million dollars tax free!

3. When everyone is finished, have players fold their treasures into tiny packets. Next, each player should put a special mark on his or her treasure—an initial or symbol—which will identify it when it is found.

4. Players must hide their treasures in the classroom—under a book, behind a table, among the leaves of a plant, under a wastepaper basket—someplace out of sight but not impossible to find.

5. After treasures are hidden, players gather back at their desks. Have them use the other sheets of paper to draw maps and clues to help other players locate their hidden treasures. Suggest that clues be kept clear and simple. For example, "Start at the door by the sink. Take three steps toward the chalkboard. Turn right and walk five steps. Look under the table." Make sure that everyone includes their secret symbol on the map so that explorers will be able to identify the proper treasure.

6. Next, have players fold maps and tear them in half. Collect both halves and put them into some type of container. Have each player select two parts. Before the search can begin, players must match the two halves of one map.

7. As treasures are found, make certain that symbols match. When a player finds a treasure that does not match, the treasure must be replaced and the search continued. The game ends when every treasure is found.

Sentence Relay

Even though this game is just for fun, it easily could be used as part of a language lesson.

Materials needed:

Chalkboard or 3 large sheets of butcher paper

3 pieces of chalk or 3 felt-tipped markers

Room arrangement:

Open space

Time:

20 minutes

Directions:

1. Draw vertical lines on the chalkboard to divide it into three sections. If no chalkboard is available, tack three large sheets of butcher paper to the wall.

2. Divide players into three teams and have them sit on the floor about six feet from their section of the chalkboard or paper.

3. Teams should arrange themselves in the order in which players will run.

4. At your command, the first member of each team races to the chalkboard or paper, picks up the chalk or marker, and writes the first word of a sentence. The player then runs back to the team and hands the chalk or marker to the next runner. This new player then writes the next word of the sentence, and so on.

5. The first team whose last player completes a full sentence with all words spelled correctly is the winner. If all team members have participated but the sentence is incomplete, the rotation begins again with the first player until the sentence is finished. Runners may correct mistakes of previous teammates while they are at the chalkboard or paper.

© McGraw-Hill Children's Publishing

0-7424-1940-1 *The Incredible Indoor Games Book*

Make a List

During the school year it is helpful to have ongoing activities—ones that can be picked up and put down at a moment's notice during a break or an in-between time when a game cannot be played. This activity becomes more and more of a challenge as it continues and yet can be available at all times.

Materials needed:

A roll of paper (brown wrapping or any large roll of paper that can be written on)

A felt-tipped marker, a crayon, or any writing implement

Tape or tacks

Room arrangement:

As is

Time:

Ongoing

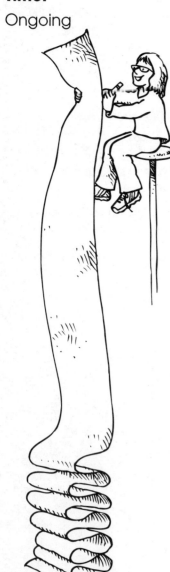

Directions:

1. Choose a free wall and tape up a large piece of paper. Find an area where it can stay up all the time so players can add to it in free moments.

2. Select a category—something that might be fun and will allow for inventive interpretations. Some examples:

   - *List things that are associated with the number 3.* Some of the things on the list might be: little pigs, blind mice, coins in a fountain, wise men, men in a tub, bears, primary colors, (red, yellow, blue), triangle, tricycle, three-ring circus, Columbus's boats, digits in an area code, or three strikes and you're out.

   - *Make a list of wet things.* Some of the things on this list might be: frog, whale, gold fish, snow, orange juice, milk, tears, dog's nose, bottom of a boat, car wash, sink, egg yolk, peache, tongue, eyeball, ink, mud, worm, pickle, perspiration, or runny nose.

   - *Make a list of little known statistics or trivial wonders.* Some people might have to go do some digging in almanacs, magazines, newspapers, or a book of world records to find things such as:

     A porcupine is equipped with about 18,000 quills; the standard 7-inch pencil will draw a line 35 miles long; Americans use a half billion hairpins a year; or Americans eat 3 billion quarts of ice cream and swallow 16 billion aspirin tablets every year.

3. Decide when and how players can add to the list. Review the list periodically as a group to point out new insights.

© McGraw-Hill Children's Publishing

0-7424-1940-1 *The Incredible Indoor Games Book*

Tongue-Tied

We've all tried tongue twisters at one time or another. You might remember "Peter Piper picked a peck of pickled peppers" or "Sally sells seashells by the seashore." Trying to say them five times fast always results in a twisted tongue, no matter how hard we try! This game gives a new twist to old twisters.

Materials needed:

Pencils

Paper

Room arrangement:

As is

Time:

20 minutes

Directions:

1. Discuss the concept of tongue twisters as a group. Most are sentences that use alliteration—beginning each word with the same letter. Some classic tongue twisters are "Rubber baby-buggy bumpers" and "Six thick thistle sticks."

2. Give each player a piece of paper and a pencil.

3. Players write a sentence making use of alliteration. Almost every word should start with the same letter. Players can use *at, the,* and *a* to help make it easier. For example: "Half the homework makes Harry happy" or "Sandy's sneakers sound scratchy on the slippery stage."

4. Players' sentences are folded and put in a container.

5. Each player randomly draws a twister and reads it out loud. See who is best at saying tongue-twisters as quickly as possible.

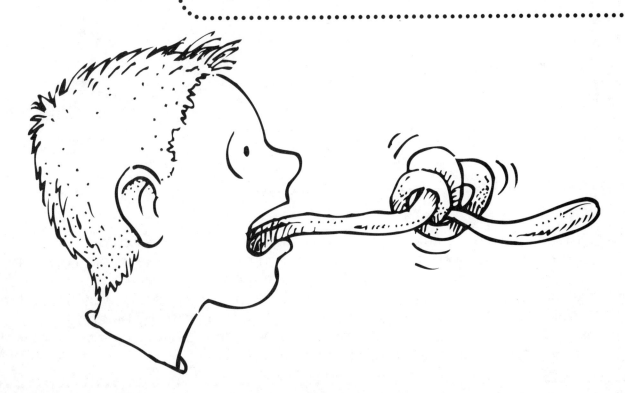

© McGraw-Hill Children's Publishing 0-7424-1940-1 *The Incredible Indoor Games Book*

Steal the Bacon

Steal the Bacon is a traditional favorite. It provides an opportunity to discuss the elements of competition and to emphasize the values of teamwork and developing strategies.

Materials needed:

A beanbag, a ball of yarn, a handkerchief, or any other object that is easy to pick up

Masking tape

Room arrangement:

Open space

Time:

25 minutes

Directions:

1. Use masking tape to make two parallel lines twelve feet apart on the floor.

2. Divide players into two teams and have them line up on the taped lines, facing each other. Have the teams count off simultaneously so that players' numbers on one team will match players on the other team.

3. The leader throws the "bacon" (beanbag or whatever) into the center between the two lines and calls out a number. Each of the two players who have that number try to retrieve the bacon and get it back across his or her team's line without being tagged by the other player. If a player is tagged before getting across the line, there is no score and the bacon is dropped where the player is tagged. If the player gets the bacon across the line, his or her team gets a point.

Variation:

To make the game a little more challenging, the leader may call out two numbers. For example, the leader calls out numbers 4 and 7. Players 4 and 7 of one team work together against 4 and 7 of the other team. If 4 grabs the bacon and is tagged, the bacon is dropped immediately and 4 may not try for it again. But 7 can still try to get the bacon and 4 can help by blocking or faking the opponents. If both members of the same side are tagged, the play is over and the bacon is left in its last position on the floor.

© McGraw-Hill Children's Publishing 0-7424-1940-1 *The Incredible Indoor Games Book*

Group Juggle

It's nothing new to see kids throwing crushed-paper balls, but encouraging it? Yikes!

Materials needed:

6 or 7 crushed
paper balls

Room arrangement:

Open space

Time:

15 minutes

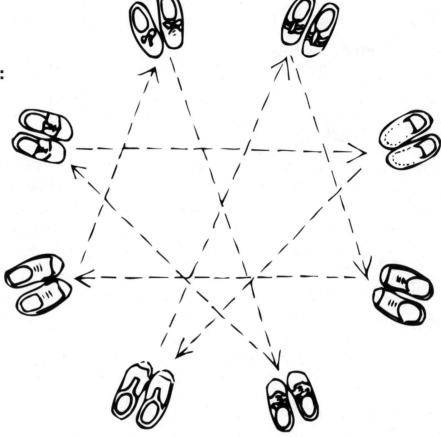

....

Directions:

1. Players stand in a circle about one arm's length apart.

2. The first player throws a crushed paper ball to someone on the other side of the circle, who throws it to a third person, and so forth. This continues until the ball makes its way to everyone once. Players are to remember to whom they throw the ball. When a pattern is set it is never broken throughout the game.

3. The leader throws the first ball. As the rhythm of the pattern becomes smoother and throwers and receivers get used to it, another ball is added, then the third, then a fourth. Players should be able, depending on the size of the group, to keep six or seven balls moving at once.

4. To help keep a steady rhythm, try having everyone sing a song, such as "Row, Row, Row Your Boat," or repeat a silly chant—"Pass the ball, not the wall!"— that keeps the beat of catching and throwing.

© McGraw-Hill Children's Publishing
0-7424-1940-1 *The Incredible Indoor Games Book*

Havaball

This indoor game demands fast reflexes and agility. It's also safe and easy to play.

Materials needed:

2 soft balls (beach balls, sponge balls, or balloons)

Room arrangement:

Open space

Time:

15 minutes

Directions:

1. Divide players into two equal teams. Teams stand in two lines facing each other and about three feet apart.

2. Alternate members of each team change places with the players opposite so that each player faces a member of the opposing team and has a member of the opposing team on either side.

3. Give a ball to each team at one end of the two lines. Each person says "Havaball" and throws or passes the ball to the team member diagonally opposite.

4. When each ball reaches the end of the line, it is passed back in the opposite direction. Passing the ball from one end of the line to the other continues as many times as agreed upon before the game. Any fumbling or dropping will slow down the passing and put the other team in the lead.

5. The first team to complete passing the ball the agreed number of rounds is the winner.

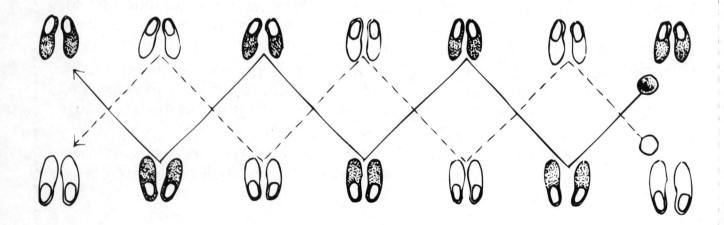

© McGraw-Hill Children's Publishing

0-7424-1940-1 *The Incredible Indoor Games Book*

Perpetual Motion

By playing this game, your group can go for a spin without leaving the room.

Materials needed:

A flying disk or a metal plate

Room arrangement:

Open space

Time:

15 minutes

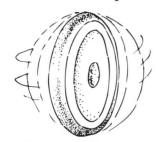

Directions:

1. Players sit in a circle on the floor and count off so that each person has a number. Place a flying disk or a metal plate on the floor in the center of the circle.

2. The first player gets up, turns the disk on edge and spins it as you would a coin. As the player sits down he or she calls out the number of another player. The player whose number is called jumps up, gets the disk before it stops, gives it another spin, and calls out another player's number before sitting down.

3. Players continue calling each other's numbers and keeping the disk spinning. If the disk completely stops spinning, a player starts it again. The object of the game is to cooperate in keeping the disk spinning, not to trick other players.

Slipped Disk

Without a doubt this game is much more fun than its name suggests.

Materials needed:

A flying disk, a plastic plate, or a metal cover

Room arrangement:

Open space

Time:

15 minutes

Directions:

1. Everyone forms a circle on hands and knees with heads facing inward.

2. An object, such as a flying disk, plastic plate, or metal cover, is placed in the middle of one person's back. The object of the game is to pass the object around the circle, from back to back, without using hands.

3. If the object falls, it is picked up by hand and placed on the back of the last person who had it. The game continues until the disk is passed successfully around the entire circle.

© McGraw-Hill Children's Publishing 0-7424-1940-1 *The Incredible Indoor Games Book*

Sounds in the Night

Late at night, animal sounds drift into the darkened house—dogs howling, crickets chirping, or cats crying. In this game, the animals are indoors and play a noisy game of ball.

Materials needed:

A beach ball or a basketball

Room arrangement:

Open space

Time:

15 minutes

Directions:

1. Everyone sits in a circle with eyes closed. The room is darkened. Each player selects an animal sound to mimic as his or her own personal signal. If group members run out of animals from which to choose, divide players into separate game groups.

2. The first player has the ball and makes his or her animal sound and then the sound of the animal to whom he or she wants to roll the ball. The animal that is "called" replies so that the first player knows where to direct the ball. The first player then rolls the ball to that animal.

3. If the intended player receives the ball, he or she responds loudly. All the other animals rejoice in unison by making their sounds also. However, if the intended player misses, the ball goes back to the first player who then tries another animal.

© McGraw-Hill Children's Publishing 0-7424-1940-1 *The Incredible Indoor Games Book*

Hot Stuff

This is a variation of Hot Potato. In the original game, the person who is caught holding the potato is out. In this game, nobody is eliminated, just rearranged.

Materials needed:

A ball or a balloon

Room arrangement:

Open space

Time:

15 minutes

Directions:

1. Move furniture and obstacles aside. Gather players in a circle.

2. One person is chosen as the Caller. Before each round, the Caller stands outside the circle and secretly picks a number from 1 to 50. As the players stand in the circle, passing the ball from player to player, the Caller counts aloud to the preselected number, and then yells "Hot stuff!"

3. Meanwhile, the players in the circle must keep the ball moving from player to player. When the Caller yells "hot stuff," the person with the ball (or if the ball is between players, the person just about to catch the ball) leaves the circle and joins the Caller.

4. As more and more players leave the circle, the Caller group becomes larger and larger, and the counting becomes louder and louder. The original Caller tells the new Callers the number to which the group will count, a different number each time.

5. As the game dwindles to two players passing the ball back and forth, the last person left without the ball when the callers yell "Hot stuff!" will be the winner.

© McGraw-Hill Children's Publishing   0-7424-1940-1 *The Incredible Indoor Games Book*

Laser Beam

In a darkened room a flashlight can become a nonlethal light saber.
Players caught in the beam before they reach home base are frozen in place.

Materials needed:

A flashlight

Room arrangement:

Open space

Time:

15 minutes

Directions:

1. The room becomes the far reaches of outer space. Darken it as much as possible by pulling window shades, covering doors, and turning off lights. One person is chosen to be the Space Patrol and stands guard over the five-foot-square space station in the center of the room with a trusty laser beam (flashlight).

2. The person who is acting as the Space Patrol closes his or her eyes and counts slowly to 50 as everyone hides. The object of the game is to try to get to the space station in the center of the room without getting tagged with the beam from the laser gun.

3. If space invaders dare to make a run to the space station and get caught by the laser beam, they are instantly frozen in space forever—or at least until the end of the game. The first person to get to the space station without getting caught is the next Space Patrol.

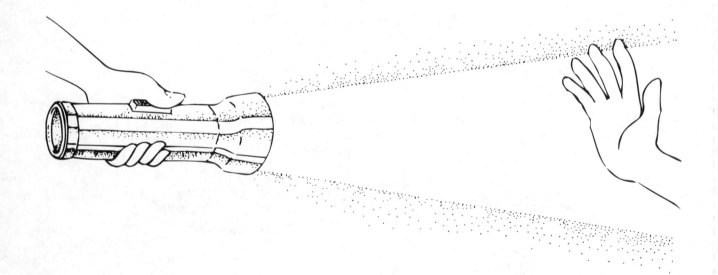

© McGraw-Hill Children's Publishing 0-7424-1940-1 *The Incredible Indoor Games Book*

Spot Check

This game is reminiscent of Pin the Tail on the Donkey without the tail or the donkey.

Materials needed:

A key, a button, a coin, or any other small object

A small pad of paper

Masking tape

A pencil for each player

Room arrangement:

Open space

Time:

15 minutes

Directions:

1. Clear the center of the room and place a small object—a key, a button, a coin, or whatever—on the floor in the center.

2. Each player writes his or her name on a small piece of paper and connects a piece of masking tape to it. At one end of the room, a starting line is marked with a line of tape.

3. One by one, players are blindfolded, turned around a few times, and told to walk to the spot where they think the object is located without actually touching the object.

4. When the player reaches the spot, he or she is allowed one chance to tape the slip of paper next to it. The game continues until each player has had a turn. The player whose paper is closest to the spot is the winner.

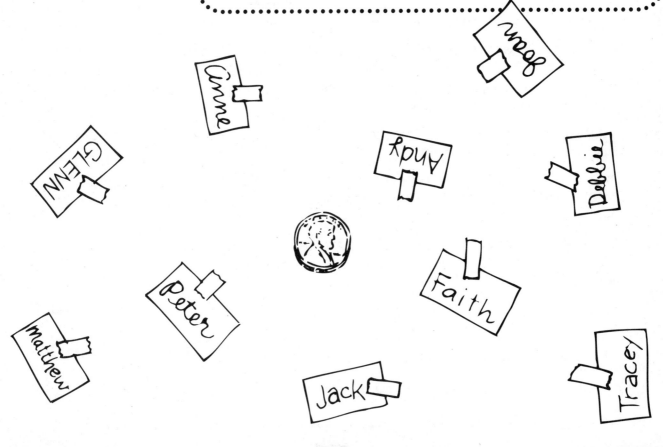

© McGraw-Hill Children's Publishing

0-7424-1940-1 *The Incredible Indoor Games Book*

Wastepaper Basketball

When the ancient Mayan game using a ball and a hoop was formalized in 1891 by Dr. James Naismith and called *basketball*, little did anyone realize that the game would be further amended by young inventors using paper balls and wastepaper baskets.

Materials needed:

2 wastepaper baskets or cardboard boxes

Crushed-paper balls

Room arrangement:

As is

Time:

25 minutes

Directions:

1. In this game, players must remain in their seats. Divide the group into two teams by counting off. Two wastepaper baskets or cardboard boxes are placed at opposite corners of the room, one for each team.

2. Players can shoot from anywhere or can pass the paper ball to each other, trying to get it to the teammate closest to the basket. Opposing team members can try to intercept shots, just as long as there is no physical contact. You can award free shots when fouls occur.

3. Referees should be stationed at each end of the room to retrieve stray paper balls and throw them back to players.

4. If the defending team intercepts a pass or retrieves the ball after a shot misses the basket, it keeps possession of the ball. After a team makes a basket, the ball goes to the other team.

5. Use a new paper ball after each basket. After an agreed-upon number of plays or amount of time, the team with the most paper balls in its basket is the winner.

Variation:

You may want to try a balloon instead of a paper ball.

© McGraw-Hill Children's Publishing   0-7424-1940-1 *The Incredible Indoor Games Book*

Balloon Soccer

Simply changing equipment and altering the rules a bit can adapt traditional outdoor games that are too vigorous for indoor play. After you've played this version of soccer, ask players to think of ways other games might be changed in order to be played safely indoors.

Materials needed:

12 balloons
(or more if you like)

2 pins

Room arrangement:

As is

Time:

25 minutes

Directions:

1. All players sit in rows evenly spaced throughout the room. Two goalies sit at opposite corners of the room. Both goalies have pushpins, safety pins, or other instruments that will break balloons. The rest of the group is divided into two teams by counting off.

2. To begin, the leader drops an inflated balloon in the center of the room. Each team tries to hit the balloon to its goalie, who remains in a corner.

3. The goalie who gets the balloon and pops it scores a point for the team. This game is also fun without keeping score. There is a great deal of status in being a balloon-popping goalie. Make sure that many players have a chance to do it.

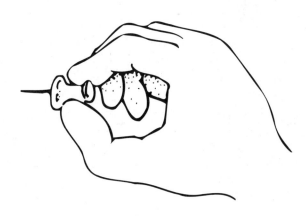

© McGraw-Hill Children's Publishing   0-7424-1940-1 *The Incredible Indoor Games Book*

Ballooning

A balloon's not much really—a bit of air wrapped in a bright package. It's not so much a toy as a possibility, an invitation to the imagination. Here are some breathtaking balloonisms.

Materials needed:

At least 1 balloon for each player

Masking tape

Room arrangement:

Open space

Time:

30 minutes

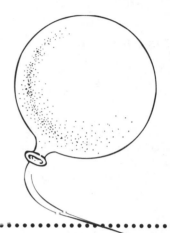

Directions:

1. Have players stand in a circle and give each player a balloon.

2. Instruct players to blow up their balloons but not tie them. Start the ballooning event with a balloon band playing "The Raspberry Serenade." (Players won't need any help in "playing" their balloons.) See if any of the balloonists can play recognizable melodies.

3. After this rousing overture, tape an *X* on the floor in the center of the circle. Players inflate balloons again but do not tie them. One by one, players release balloons, seeing how close each can come to the *X*.

4. Players retrieve balloons and tape a boundary line on either side of the room. For this part of the activity, inflate five balloons and tie them. Divide the group into five teams. All teams line up single file behind one of the boundaries. This is a balloon relay game. The first member of each team is given a balloon. At the leader's signal, the players must bat their balloons across the room and back again to the next team member in line. If a balloon touches the floor, the player must go back and start from the beginning. The first team to finish is the winner.

5. Next, have players inflate and tie all the balloons. The leader gathers all the balloons in one corner and, one by one, tosses them to the group. The group must not let any balloon touch the floor. For an added challenge, suggest that players not use their hands.

6. To end with a big blast, allow players to sit on their balloons and pop them all at once.

© McGraw-Hill Children's Publishing   0-7424-1940-1 *The Incredible Indoor Games Book*

Balloon Ball for All

Everyone has a ball dancing at the Balloon Ball!

Materials needed:

Balloons

Music

Room arrangement:

Open space

Time:

10 minutes

Directions:

1. Divide players into groups of three.

2. Give one balloon to each group. Two of the three players keep the balloon, leaving one player without one.

3. Without using hands, the two players with the balloon use it to connect together. This is done by squeezing the balloon between them to link heads, stomachs, sides, legs, etc.

4. When the music begins, players linked by balloons begin to move around the room in a silly dance rhythm. The odd players without balloons roam the room and try to find partners. The trick is to give your balloon away to two balloonless players without using your hands. To encourage switching, a leader might yell, "Switch-a-roo!" like at a square dance.

5. After a few lively songs, the balloon dancers may want to try the ultimate Balloon Ball challenge and connect the entire group together in a line with balloons linking everyone together.

The Ghost Game

How many players could recognize the spirit of a friend who returned as a ghost? Here's a chance to find out.

Materials needed:

An old bed sheet or large piece of fabric

Room arrangement:

Open space

Time:

15 minutes

Directions:

1. Divide the group into two teams.

2. One team is chosen to leave the room and send back one of its members draped in a sheet.

3. The "ghost" should try to augment the disguise by crouching to look smaller or stretching to look taller or wider. Make sure that nothing is visible (shoes or pants) to give the ghost's identity away.

4. The guessing team cannot touch the ghost. After a short consultation, the team is allowed one chance to guess the ghost's identity.

5. If the guess is wrong, another ghost from the same team comes in. If the guess is correct, the two teams switch places.

© McGraw-Hill Children's Publishing

One-Act Plays

Every now and then you may need a quick activity that takes very little explanation and can be performed in minutes. Each of these three activities can be done in less than five minutes.

Materials needed:

A nickel

A potato chip, a piece of popcorn, or a piece of soft candy

2 peanuts

Masking tape

Room arrangement:

Open space

Time:

Less than 5 minutes each

Directions:

Nickel Nose

Borrow a nickel and ask a volunteer to lie down on the floor. Place the nickel on the person's nose and tell him or her to wiggle the nickel off by wrinkling nose and face. No head movements are allowed for this nearly impossible act.

Chip Away

Place a potato chip, piece of popcorn, or small piece of candy on a player's shoulder. The player must remove the morsel with his or her tongue.

Nosed Out

Select two players to have a race by rolling peanuts across the floor with their noses. Put lines of tape on the floor for the start and finish. In this game, the winner always wins by a nose.

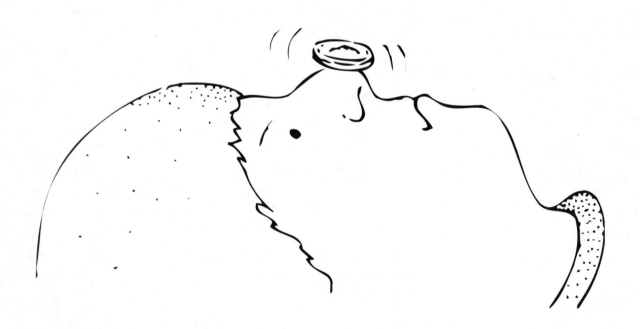

© McGraw-Hill Children's Publishing 0-7424-1940-1 *The Incredible Indoor Games Book*

World Champion Paper-Stacking Contest

Skyscrapers are exciting symbols of human ability and imagination.
This skyscraping activity requires plenty of both.

Materials needed:

As much scrap paper as possible

Room arrangement:

Open space

Time:

20–30 minutes

Directions:

1. Clear a large, open space in the room. Divide the group into two teams or into several small ones.

2. Each team gets an equal pile of paper with which to build a tower. Papers should be folded to reinforce construction. The tighter the paper is folded, the stronger it gets—but it also gets smaller. Loosely folded paper might provide larger building elements, but the construction will be more fragile.

3. The team that builds the highest tower wins an award. Also award citations for the most clever construction techniques and the most beautiful towers.

Variation:

Have the entire group work together to build the world's largest paper building.

© McGraw-Hill Children's Publishing

0-7424-1940-1 *The Incredible Indoor Games Book*

Pipe Line

People have smoked pipes, had pipe dreams, and even followed pied pipers. Now, here's a pipe game to play.

Materials needed:

A sheet of 9" x 12" construction paper for each player

2 paper clips for each player

2 small crushed paper balls or any 2 small round objects

Room arrangement:

Open space

Time:

10 minutes

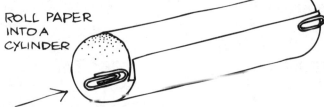

ROLL PAPER INTO A CYLINDER

FASTEN ENDS WITH PAPER CLIPS

Directions:

1. Give each person a sheet of construction paper and two paper clips. Have players roll their papers into 12-inch cylinders with a 1-inch overlap. Fasten ends with paper clips.

2. Separate the group into two teams and have them stand in two parallel lines. Tell teams to hold their paper cylinders end to end to create a long pipe.

3. Crush two pieces of paper into balls small enough to fit through the cylinders. Say "Go!" and drop the paper balls into the ends of the first two cylinders. Team members must jiggle the paper balls from one cylinder to the next. If a paper ball drops on the floor, the last person must pick it up and try again. Passes can only be made from cylinder to cylinder.

4. When the paper ball gets to the last person's cylinder, teams must reverse the passing. The first team to get the paper ball back to the beginning is the winner.

© McGraw-Hill Children's Publishing   0-7424-1940-1 *The Incredible Indoor Games Book*

Newspaper Relay

This is not a game in which to be footloose and fancy-free but rather to be as surefooted as possible.

Materials needed:

Newspapers

Room arrangement:

Open space

Time:

20 minutes

Directions:

1. Divide the group into two teams.

2. Fold several sheets of newspaper into quarters to create a solid pad on which to step. Each team will need two pads.

3. Give the first person on each team two folded newspaper pads.

4. Define the starting line behind which teams must stand. Select a goal across the room.

5. When the leader signals, the first player on each team must put down a newspaper pad and step on it, then put down the other newspaper pad and step on that one, then pick up the first and put it farther ahead to step on, and so on, until the player reaches the goal. The process is repeated on the return trip.

6. Upon returning, the first player touches the next player in line. The next player continues in the same fashion.

7. The first team to finish wins the relay.

133

© McGraw-Hill Children's Publishing

Rope Relay

This is the kind of game in which being a slippery character pays off!

Materials needed:

Two 3' pieces of rope or heavy yarn

Room arrangement:

Open space

Time:

15 minutes

Directions:

1. Tie ropes into loops to fit over the biggest player in the group.

2. Divide the group into two lines. Each line is a team. To add some team spirit, have each line pick a name, such as the Super Loopers or the Silver Slippers.

3. Give the first person on each team a rope loop. The object of the game is to have each person slip through the loop and pass it along for each of the following players to slip though.

4. A referee should make sure everyone goes through. The first team that gets everyone through the loop is the winner.

© McGraw-Hill Children's Publishing 0-7424-1940-1 *The Incredible Indoor Games Book*

Kangaroo Relay

Players will jump for joy when you ask them to hop to it in this game.

Materials needed:

A chair

A basketball, a beach ball, or a balloon

Room arrangement:

Open space

Time:

10 minutes

Directions:

1. Divide the group into two teams and have players line up, one behind the other. Place a chair about ten feet in front of each team.

2. The first players place a ball between their knees, hop to and around the chair, and return to tag the next players in line. Players may touch the ball with their hands to pass it to the next player or to pick it up when dropped, but they cannot move while touching the ball with their hands.

3. The first team to send every member around the chair and back is the winner.

© McGraw-Hill Children's Publishing

Spinning a Yarn

Here's a game that will transform a room of players into a closely knit group.

Materials needed:

A ball of thick yarn

Room arrangement:

Open space

Time:

5–10 minutes

Directions:

1. Players stand together randomly in a group.

2. One player takes a ball of thick yarn, wraps the end around his or her waist, and then passes the ball to another person.

3. The next player wraps it around his or her waist and continues to pass the ball of yarn to another player, and so forth.

4. Once the entire group has been all bound up in the yarn, the whole group process is reversed, but this time players close their eyes. The last player unwraps himself or herself, rewinds the ball, and hands it to the next player, and so on, until the rewound ball reaches the first player again.

© McGraw-Hill Children's Publishing 0-7424-1940-1 *The Incredible Indoor Games Book*

Force Field

An entire group is trapped inside the electric force field. Will they be able to work together in a spirit of cooperation and escape? Tune in to this game to find out!

Materials needed:

20' to 30' of clothesline rope

Broom

Chair or desk

Room arrangement:

Open space

Time:

20 minutes

Directions:

1. Divide a room in half by tying a rope from one side to the other, about three feet off the floor. Gather the entire group on one side of the rope.

2. The rope represents an electric force field. Players who accidentally touch it are zapped with electricity, must fall to the floor, and must remain there for the rest of the game. The object of the game is to get everyone from one side of the fence to the other without getting zapped.

3. This problem demands group cooperation. Players cannot jump over or crawl under the force field. Instead, they must work together to carefully lift each other over the force field. To help, only one object can be used—a chair or desk to stand on or a broom held by players on either side to assist the climb. Be careful that players do not throw each other over the force field and that the last person doesn't dive over it.

Variation:

For older children it's fun to play Force Field in total silence as if it were a secret escape. Players will have to pantomime instructions to each other.

© McGraw-Hill Children's Publishing

Stringing Along

This game will strike a positive cord. Players will need sharp vision, nimble fingers, and a thread of hope.

Materials needed:

A ball of string

Scissors

Room arrangement:

As is

Time:

15 minutes

Directions:

1. Cut 75 to 100 pieces of string of varying lengths—from two inches to several feet. Hide each piece of string someplace in the room before players arrive.

2. Have players stand in the middle of the room. Divide the group into two teams and explain that you've hidden pieces of string, pointing out the most obvious ones.

3. The object of the game is for each team to find and tie together as many strings as possible. Since the strings are not the same length, the winning team will not necessarily be the one with the largest number of strings but the one with the longest line.

4. When it seems that most strings have been found and tied, have teams stretch their lines of string next to each other to compare. The team with the longest string is the winner.

© McGraw-Hill Children's Publishing   0-7424-1940-1 *The Incredible Indoor Games Book*

Throw Shows

Many games involve throwing a ball, bean bag, or water balloon. Propelling such substantial objects can be dangerous indoors. Here are some throwing alternatives that are safely suitable for small spaces.

Materials needed:

Cloth

Soda straws

Paper plates

Balloons

Room arrangement:

Open space

Time:

20 minutes

Directions:

1. Select a soft object to throw, such as napkin-sized cloths, plastic soda straws, paper plates, or balloons.

2. The object of a throwing game is either distance or accuracy—or both. First, you need to decide on the objective. You may want to aim for a defined target such as a hoop or a big box or you may want to see whose object flies the farthest. Players should throw from behind a defined line. Test-toss materials to determine a fair size for the playing field.

3. Now players are ready to toss.

   - *Napkin-sized cloths:* Players may want to crumple the cloth to give it some mass but may not fold it or tie it in a knot. Cloth tosses are difficult because the fabric inflates with air and tends to float toward the ground.

   - *Paper plates:* With a flick of a wrist, a paper plate can turn into a flying disc and may end up sailing too long for the room. Suspending a hoop or some sort of frame from the ceiling will provide a target.

   - *Plastic soda straws:* Soda straws can be thrown like miniature spears. Each player may want to use a marker to decorate her or his straw. Players line up in a row and, at the count of three, throw their "spears" across the room. The leader can retrieve the three farthest throws and identify the players from their markings.

   - *Balloons:* No water balloons here! We're strictly full of air. Balloons can be kicked, blown, or knocked into the air. Since they are hard to control, accuracy may be frustrating, so measuring distance may be the way to go.

© McGraw-Hill Children's Publishing 0-7424-1940-1 *The Incredible Indoor Games Book*

Multiple Hopscotch

Those who always avoid stepping on cracks so as not to break Mother's back will probably like Multiple Hopscotch. These three hopscotch grids are easy to make and the games presented can be changed to fit specific groups. Children may play on them without any outside organization. A plus: the grids look very nice when they are not being used.

Materials needed:

3 to 6 rolls of masking tape for each board

Scissors

A tape measure or yardstick

Chalk or pencil

Room arrangement:

Open space

Time:

60 minutes to construct a game grid
10 minutes for group activities

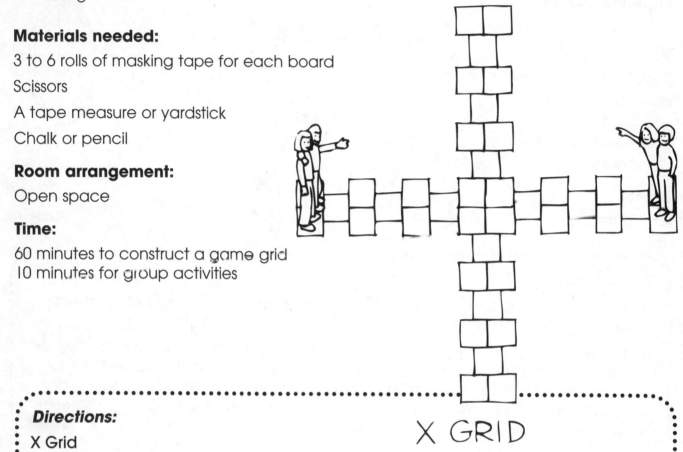

X GRID

Directions:

X Grid

1. Tape the grid on the floor.

2. Divide the group into two teams. Divide team members into pairs.

3. The first two pairs stand arm in arm on the double squares at opposite ends of the board. Each player stands on one foot. The object of the game is to hop to the middle, one square at a time, then turn right and hop down the other arm of the game board.

4. When you say "Go," the two pairs hop toward the center. The first pair to reach the center gets to use the four middle squares first in order to turn while the other team waits.

5. After both pairs pass the center and are hopping down opposite arms, the next pairs of hoppers can go. The first team to get all team members to the end is the winner.

© McGraw-Hill Children's Publishing 0-7424-1940-1 *The Incredible Indoor Games Book*

Multiple Hopscotch (cont.)

Woven Grid

1. Tape the grid on the floor.

2. Divide the group into four teams. Each team picks a side of the game board. The object of the game is to hop on one foot from one side of the game board to the other and then reassemble the team. Large teams may have to take two separate turns.

3. When you say "Go," everyone starts to hop through the grid, trying not to bump into other players. To make hopping routes more of a challenge, certain squares can be marked out of bounds with colored paper or tape.

4. The first team to reassemble on the opposite side is the winner.

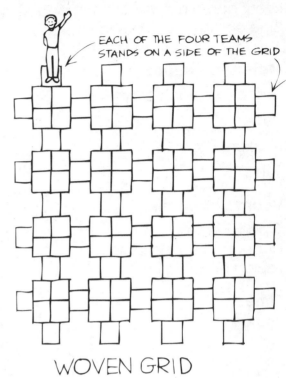

EACH OF THE FOUR TEAMS STANDS ON A SIDE OF THE GRID

WOVEN GRID

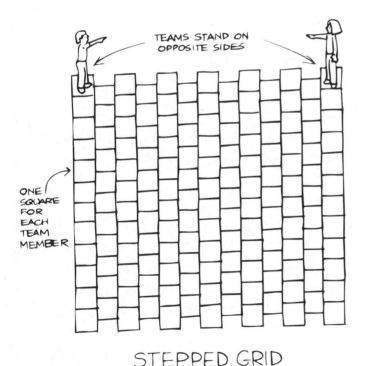

TEAMS STAND ON OPPOSITE SIDES

ONE SQUARE FOR EACH TEAM MEMBER

STEPPED GRID

Stepped Grid

1. Tape the grid on the floor. The squares on two opposite sides should add up to enough spaces for the entire group.

2. Divide the group into two teams, one team standing on one side of the grid and the other team on the opposite side.

3. When you say "Go," both teams hop across the grid to the opposite side, each player on one foot, without bumping into other players.

4. Players who hop into a square with another player already in it will have to go back and start over.

5. The first team to reassemble on the opposite side wins.

© McGraw-Hill Children's Publishing

0-7424-1940-1 *The Incredible Indoor Games Book*

Circular Musical Chairs

Every game has its variation and Musical Chairs is no exception.
One of my favorite variations does not remove chairs. It just keeps players.

Materials needed:

A chair for each player

Paper

Markers

Tape

Room arrangement:

Open space with chairs
arranged in a circle
facing outward

Time:

10 minutes

Directions:

1. Each player has a chair; chairs are arranged in a circle facing outward. Each player writes his or her name on a sheet of paper and tapes it to the chair.

2. The game begins with all players taking their seats and memorizing their positions.

3. When the music begins, players march left or right (leader's choice) around the chairs.

4. When the music stops, players must scramble for their own chairs. The last to reach his or her chair pays the penalty by sitting in that chair for the rest of the game (players remaining seated must tuck their feet beneath their chairs and keep their hands in their laps).

5. As the game continues, direct players to march in various manners—hopping, skipping, about-face, etc. Everyone must stay in line and keep moving. Players should not hover near their chairs.

6. Eventually, only two people will be left standing. The first person back to his or her chair is the winner.

Spooling Around

This game may string you along, but just think of it as a fun way to unwind.

Materials needed:

2 spools of string or yarn about 25' long

Room arrangement:

Tables, chairs, and other obstacles

Time:

30–45 minutes

Directions:

1. Divide players into teams of two.

2. Define a course that goes under tables, around corners, over chairs, and possibly through several rooms or spaces, such as down a hallway.

3. Give each team a ball of yarn, thread, or string. Tie each string to a solid object, such as a table leg or door knob.

4. This is a type of relay race. The first two members of the opposing teams start on the word "Go!" They must unravel their string and wind it around objects as they negotiate their way through the course. Each team, crawling under tables and around chairs and corners, must twist its string around the same number of objects.

5. Each player arrives at the end of the course (in a small room it may be the beginning of the course) and hands the spool over to his or her teammate.

6. The teammate must carefully roll the string back up on the spool. If the string is not rolled, or if it is broken, they lose the race.

7. The first team back to the starting line is the winner. Once two teams have completed the course, the next two teams begin. The winners of each team may want to have a playoff to determine the champions.

Variation:

If things get too hectic with two racers on the same course at one time, try creating two identical courses. Or, only allow one team on the course at a time and use a stopwatch to time the event. This will alleviate the need for playoffs, unless two teams complete the course in exactly the same amount of time.

© McGraw-Hill Children's Publishing 0-7424-1940-1 *The Incredible Indoor Games Book*

Now You See Them, Now You Don't

Our eyes often deceive us and what we think we saw is not always actually what we saw. This game tests our abilities to perceive a situation and remember it exactly.

Materials needed:

Dress-up clothes—shirts, hats, gloves, overalls, etc.

Room arrangement:

As is

Time:

15 minutes

Directions:

1. Six or more players are chosen to leave the room.

2. Out of sight of the rest of the group, the six players put on some of the dress-up clothes. When everyone is ready, the six players run quickly in and out of the room in a particular formation.

3. The six players come back into the room out of formation with the dress-up clothes removed. The rest of the group must rearrange the runners in the order they appeared when they made their quick entrance and exit.

4. After the group agrees on the formation they believe they saw, the runners make any necessary corrections.

© McGraw-Hill Children's Publishing 0-7424-1940-1 *The Incredible Indoor Games Book*

New Odds

It's amazing how much fun a standard childhood game can be when a few changes make it almost new again. In the traditional game of Odds and Evens, players quickly raise and lower their fists three times before they call out, "Odd" or, "Even," and show one or two fingers. If the total is three fingers, the person calling out "Odd" is the winner. If two or four fingers are showing, the "Even" caller is the winner. In case both players make the same call, it's a tie. Although players still like this unadorned version, here's an odd way to make it even more fun.

Materials needed:

Dress-up clothes—shirts, hats, gloves, overalls, etc.

Room arrangement:

Open space

Time:

10 minutes

Directions:

1. Have the players pair up. Practice the traditional game of Odds and Evens several times.

2. Each pair of players is limited to ten "throws." The winner of the throw directs the loser to wear one silly dress-up item.

3. If a person whose appearance has been changed wins a throw, he or she can either remove one dress-up item or instruct the other player to wear one silly dress-up item.

4. At the end of ten throws, the player with the fewest additional items of clothing is the winner. Players can switch partners and begin again.

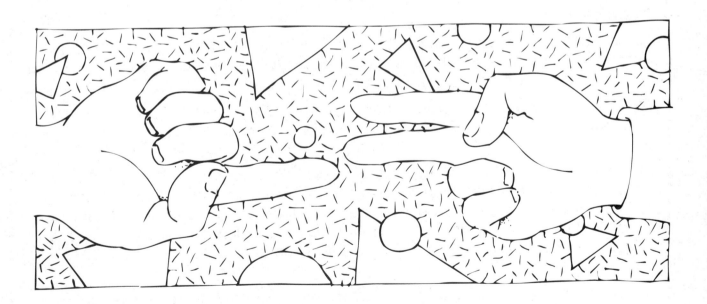

© McGraw-Hill Children's Publishing 0-7424-1940-1 *The Incredible Indoor Games Book*

Bread Paintings

Here's an activity that is not only fun to do but good to eat. Bread paintings can transform any everyday sandwich into a work of art using materials found in almost any kitchen.

Materials needed:

2 slices of white bread for each player

Assorted food colorings

2 quarts of milk

A paper cup for each player

A new watercolor paintbrush for each player or a supply of cotton-tipped swabs

Toaster

Room arrangement:

Individual work areas for each group of five or six players

Time:

30–40 minutes

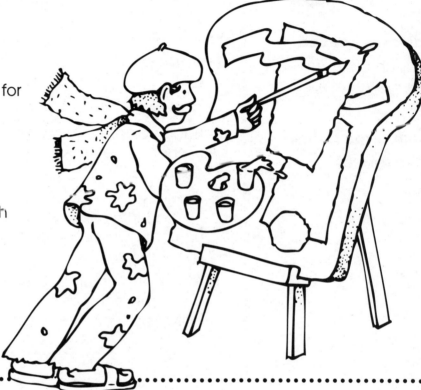

Directions:

1. Have the players form groups of five or six. Supply each group with five or six paper cups containing small amounts of milk. Add a little food coloring to each cup of milk. Give each player two slices of bread.

2. Players should use new brushes or cotton-tipped swabs to apply the milk-paint. To keep colors bright, tell players to keep brushes separate and not to mix colors.

3. This is a good project to experiment with different painting styles. Try scribbling a design with one color, then fill in the spaces with other colors and patterns. Brush stripes in one direction with one color, then brush stripes of another color at right angles to create a plaid pattern. Draw pictures of stars and rainbows, or just cover the bread with multicolored dots. Be careful not to get bread too soaked with milk.

4. Dry the bread paintings in a toaster set for light toast. When everyone has finished making edible art, other transformations will happen with each bite.

© McGraw-Hill Children's Publishing   0-7424-1940-1 *The Incredible Indoor Games Book*

Snack-Food Sculpture

The history of snack food as we know it probably began with the first television commercial, when millions of people ran to their kitchens in search of fast treats—and back in time for the rest of the show. While doing this activity, players build more than just an appetite.

Materials needed:

4 or 5 different kinds of snack food (bread sticks, pretzels, rippled potato chips, corn chips, cheese curls, popcorn, crackers, and so forth)

Three 8-ounce packages of cream cheese

An 8-ounce container of sour cream

A package of dried onion soup mix

Mixing bowl

Mixing spoon

A plastic knife for each player

A paper plate for each player

Room arrangement:

As is

Time:

30–40 minutes

Fabulous!

Directions:

1. Before making snack-food sculptures, prepare the "paste" to stick pieces together. Mix three 8-ounce packages of softened cream cheese with 8 ounces of sour cream. Blend in a package of dried onion soup mix.

2. Divide the players into groups of five or six. Give each group an assortment of snack foods—bread sticks, pretzels, crackers, and so forth—and some paste. Each player should have a paper plate and a plastic knife.

3. Before pasting the snack food together with the onion soup mixture, lay out pieces on the paper plates as a framework for construction. Snack foods such as bread sticks, pretzels, crackers, and rippled potato chips are structurally sound and are good for foundations. To build a tall structure, use bread sticks as a skeleton and add lighter foods, such as cheese curls, on top.

4. If the finished basic structure seems strong enough, decorate the surface with popcorn, crackers, and taco chips. Try repeating a row of cheese puffs across the top or sticking pretzel bits out from the sides.

5. When snack-food sculptures are finished, they should be displayed. Organize a snack-food parade with the sculptures as floats. At parade's end, snack-food sculptures can be eaten—artfully nibbled into nothingness.

© McGraw-Hill Children's Publishing 0-7424-1940-1 *The Incredible Indoor Games Book*

Foiling Around

Aluminum foil is very practical—and it's also a lot of fun.
In this activity, players won't mind being foolish.

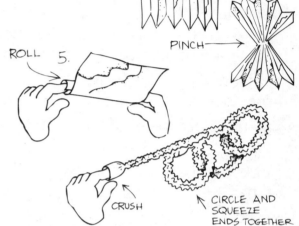

Materials needed:

Roll of heavy-duty aluminum foil

Scissors

Cellophane tape

Medium-weight string

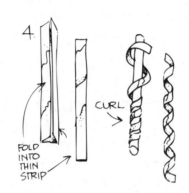

Room arrangement:

As is

Time:

30 minutes

Directions:

1. Tie several pieces of medium-weight string across the room to hang decorations as they are completed.

2. Give each player a three-foot sheet of foil. Players can share scissors and cellophane tape.

3. Aluminum foil fans are made by cutting a rectangle of foil approximately 9" x 12", folding it into an accordion, and pinching the center together.

4. Curls are made by first folding a long sheet of foil into a thin strip, then twisting the strip around a broom handle or dowel. Remove the molded curl.

5. Foil chains are fun to construct with several players. Cut some foil into 8-inch squares. Roll up a square into a long thin stick, holding one end open with a finger. Form the foil stick into a circle, slipping the slender end into the open end and then crushing them together. Continue to connect foil circles into a long chain that can loop across the ceiling.

6. A Chinese lantern is a bit more complicated. Fold a 12" x 20" sheet of foil in half the long way. Place a sheet of paper between the folded halves (for cutting ease) and cut in from the folded side an inch or so apart. Only cut to about 1" from the outer edges. Remove the sheet of paper and unfold the foil. Tape the ends together to form a circle. Tape a strip of foil across one of the ends to form a handle so the lantern can be hung from the string.

7. Encourage players to crush foil scraps into any and all sorts of shapes. For added effects, turn a rotating, colored spotlight on the foil decorations and turn off overhead lights.

© McGraw-Hill Children's Publishing   0-7424-1940-1 *The Incredible Indoor Games Book*

Foiled Again!

Students will really be able to get into this activity as they mold full-scale portraits of each other with aluminum foil.

Materials needed:

Rolls of heavy-duty aluminum foil

Scissors

Cellophane tape

Room arrangement:

Open space

Time:

30 minutes

Directions:

1. Before players begin, cut two sheets of foil about five feet long for each player.

2. Separate the group into pairs. Each player should tape the two sheets of foil together along one of the long sides of each sheet to have a sheet wide enough to cover a single person.

3. One player of each pair lies on the floor. The other player places the sheet over his or her supine partner, carefully molding the foil around arms, legs, torso, and head. Extra care should be given when molding around the head to avoid hurting the person under the foil.

4. Foil should be lifted off carefully. Excess foil can be trimmed away with scissors. Scraps should be saved for future foil sculptures. Then the partners should switch so that molds of both players are made.

5. Foil figures can be hung with string from the ceiling or tacked directly to the wall. Try molding several players at once into a three-headed, six-legged, six-armed monster. Foil figures add a glamorous gallery of glittering ghosts to gloomy rooms.

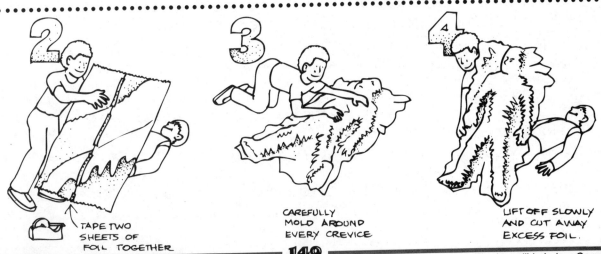

TAPE TWO SHEETS OF FOIL TOGETHER

CAREFULLY MOLD AROUND EVERY CREVICE

LIFT OFF SLOWLY AND CUT AWAY EXCESS FOIL.

© McGraw-Hill Children's Publishing

0-7424-1940-1 *The Incredible Indoor Games Book*

Group Loop

Some activities tie people together more than other activities.
This one bands them together and springs them into action.

Materials needed:

Bolt of fabric, 10 to 15 yards long

Room arrangement:

Open space

Time:

15 minutes

Directions:

1. Securely tie the ends of the long bolt of fabric together so that it forms a large loop.

2. Have players step inside the loop and face the center, spacing themselves equally and pulling the loop up behind them. Players should step back and lean on the inside of the fabric, stretching it taut enough to support everyone.

3. With the fabric stretched tightly, have players roll slowly against it in one direction, then reverse and roll the opposite way.

4. Divide the group into four sections. The two sections across from each other release the fabric and switch places. As the fabric is released, the other two groups stretch the fabric to take up the slack. As the two teams reassemble and lean on the fabric again, it will stretch and the other two sections will be drawn toward the center. The two teams across from each other alternate with the other two teams that face each other, beginning slowly to set up a rhythm of switch and stretch.

© McGraw-Hill Children's Publishing 0-7424-1940-1 *The Incredible Indoor Games Book*

Wrap-Ups

Children often like to decorate themselves in the most outlandish ways. Dressing up in unusual ways helps them to feel like brand-new people. This is an activity that will really get them in shape.

Materials needed:

Fabric scraps

String or yarn

Room arrangement:

Open space

Time:

30 minutes

Directions:

1. For this game, collect as many fabric scraps as you can—the more the better.

2. Push all the furniture to the corners of the room to create an open space. Place the fabric scraps and the string in the center of the space.

3. Have each person pick a body part to transform using fabric scraps. To get started, suggest that they can wrap and stuff fabric to create cone heads, huge clown feet, great muscular arms, and bulging stomachs. Fabric might be wrapped around limbs or tied on with string. Coats and jackets can be worn over new body shapes to complete the transformation.

4. After these creatures have been created, organize a parade through the room, or ask the children to dance a slow-motion ballet.

© McGraw-Hill Children's Publishing 0-7424-1940-1 *The Incredible Indoor Games Book*

Banner Together

Banners are often used to proclaim the identity of individuals or groups. This activity allows individuals to express themselves by collaborating to make a group banner.

Materials needed:

Assorted-colored felt rectangles approximately 9" x 12", one for each player

Fabric scraps, leftover ribbing, sequins, buttons, and so forth

Scissors

White glue

Assorted colored felt-tipped markers

Stapler

Safety pins

40" dowel or wood strip

Room arrangement:

Work area for every five or six players

Time:

40–60 minutes

TACK BANNER TO A PIECE OF WOOD AND HANG WITH SCREW EYES AND STRING

STAPLE OR PIN FELT PIECES TOGETHER

Directions:

1. Before the activity begins, cover work tables with newspaper. Divide the players into groups of five or six. Give each player a felt rectangle. Supply each group with several pairs of scissors, a container or two of white glue, a few felt-tipped markers, and an assortment of fabric scraps and other decorative materials.

2. Since this banner is a symbol of the group as a whole, each person should be free to make a picture or design that expresses his or her own feelings and ideas. One may want to make an intricate design with lots of small details while another may want to make a very literal picture of some object. Whatever players decide on, they must cut it out of materials available and glue it to their felt rectangles. Felt-tipped markers should be used for outlining, highlighting, and adding mottoes.

3. Staple several felt pieces in a row. When several equal rows of felt rectangles are connected, finish assembling them into a larger banner with safety pins. To hang the banner, staple or tack one end to a wooden dowel or piece of wood.

4. After the banner is finished, hang it from the ceiling or against the wall. The group can use the banner to head special parades and show off group spirit.

© McGraw-Hill Children's Publishing 0-7424-1940-1 *The Incredible Indoor Games Book*

Outer Faces

Our faces tell many stories. In this activity, your group can enlarge on facial communication with the help of a little theatrical makeup.

Materials needed:

Bottles of assorted-color water-based theatrical makeup

Plastic cups for makeup and water

Small inexpensive brushes or a supply of cotton-tipped swabs

Mirrors

Cold cream

Room arrangement:

Groups of five chairs

Time:

45 minutes

Directions:

1. Divide the players into groups of five. Give each group a cup and a brush or a swab for each makeup color. Pour one-fourth inch of makeup into each cup. Although this activity is easy to motivate, it can become disorganized if not supervised. Try to get players to keep colors and brushes separated or colors will become muddy.

2. Before players begin to transform themselves, they must decide on expressions to paint on their faces—happy, sad, angry, surprised, scared, and so on. Players must not tell each other which expression they have chosen. You can help players by discussing expressions, how each one is different and what each one communicates—furrowed brows, wrinkled noses, and so forth. Have them experiment by making faces in a mirror.

3. After face painters are finished, seat them in a circle on the floor. One by one, players show off their faces and may even act out the emotion they are intending to communicate. This is a good opportunity for everyone to ham it up.

4. After the activity has ended, players should have the option to keep the makeup on or to wash it off. Theatrical makeup will dry and should not come off on furniture but may rub off on clothing.

Tips:

- This activity works best when there are parent volunteers or classroom aides to help monitor the mess.

- Makeup will wash off more easily if players apply cold cream before applying the makeup.

© McGraw-Hill Children's Publishing

Mammoth Murals

Every good production depends on its set designers to come up with an innovative and creative look. With an overhead projector to help create a large, collaborative mural, young artists will be able to produce a masterpiece faster than you can say "Pop art!" A completed mural may be used later as a backdrop for video or live-performance productions.

Materials needed:

A sheet of 8 1/2" x 11" paper for each player

A pencil for each player

Assorted colored felt-tipped markers or crayons

Masking tape

An overhead projector

Photocopy-compatible transparency

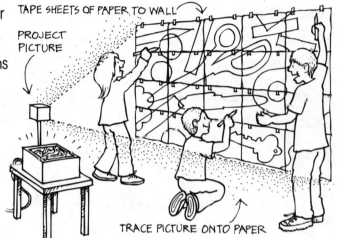

TAPE SHEETS OF PAPER TO WALL

PROJECT PICTURE

TRACE PICTURE ONTO PAPER

Room arrangement:

Open space with a large, blunk wall

Time:

45 minutes

Directions:

1. You'll need a black-and-white line drawing to photocopy on a transparency. The image should be filled with lots of tiny details. There are several ways to find an image, such as coloring books or old prints and etchings. Or, you can draw your own.

2. If you choose to make a drawing, simply take a letter-sized piece of paper and trace handy objects, overlapping them into a design. You might trace your hand, scissors, pencils, coins, or any other small objects.

3. After you've prepared your transparency, place it on an overhead projector and project the image on a large wall or whiteboard. Adjust the projector so that the image is as big and sharp as possible.

4. Cover the area being projected with a gridwork of paper sheets, tacking the edges with small pieces of tape. Each person should have at least one piece of paper to color. If you have a large group, you may need to do several murals in a few shifts.

5. Each person should trace his or her portion of the projected image with a pencil. Remind artists not to add extra lines.

6. After completing the tracing, artists carefully remove their papers from the wall and begin filling their lines by adding colors with markers or crayons.

7. When everyone is finished, reassemble the mural, replacing the sheets in their original order. The result will be a mammoth surprise for everyone.

Shadow Shapes

In this activity, players become shady characters doing gymnastics to help their shadows get in shape.

Materials needed:

Large roll of white paper (at least 36" wide)

Thumb tacks or masking tape

Assorted-color felt-tipped markers

Assorted-color tempera paint

Brushes

Bucket of water

4 to 6 spotlights or the light from an overhead projector

Room arrangement:

Open wall space

Time:

35–45 minutes

PAIRS OF PLAYERS TRACE EACH OTHER'S SHADOWS

Directions:

1. Tack or tape a roll of white paper across the wall. Pull shades and close doors to make the room as dark as possible. Plug in spotlights or an overhead projector and direct the light toward the paper.

2. Divide the group into pairs. Partners take turns tracing each other's shadows with felt-tipped markers on the white paper. Players should turn, stretch, and crouch to see how many different shapes they can make with their bodies. Several players can stand together to merge silhouettes.

3. Spotlights can be moved to elongate, enlarge, or shrink shapes. For example, finger shadows can stretch out several feet across the wall. Suggest players trace the same shadow shape several times, overlapping it in different colors.

FILL IN SHAPES WITH COLORS AND PATTERNS

4. Players fill in the shapes with solid colors of tempera paint or with patterns such as stars, checks, stripes, dots, and so forth.

© McGraw-Hill Children's Publishing 0-7424-1940-1 *The Incredible Indoor Games Book*

Jam Session

You don't have to own a fancy grand piano or play the guitar to be a musician. In this activity, common everyday materials become instrumental in a do-it-yourself orchestra.

Materials needed:

Wooden dowels, 3' long, 1/2" diameter

Hand saw

Heavy cardboard tubes

Blocks of wood, 2" x 4" x 6"

Sheets of medium-weight sandpaper

White glue

Small boxes with lids

Paper lunch bags

Rubber bands

An assortment of beads, buttons, pebbles, marbles, and so on

RHYTHM BLOCKS
Glue sandpaper to
two pieces of wood
and rub together

Room arrangement:

As is

Time:

45–60 minutes

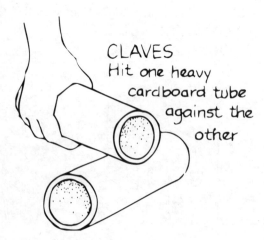

CLAVES
Hit one heavy
cardboard tube
against the
other

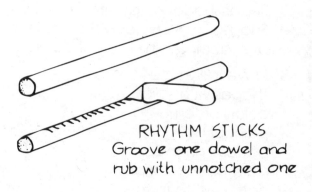

RHYTHM STICKS
Groove one dowel and
rub with unnotched one

© McGraw-Hill Children's Publishing

0-7424-1940-1 *The Incredible Indoor Games Book*

Jam Session (cont.)

Directions:

1. Gather materials on a table. These simple instruments can be made quickly.

   - *Rhythm Sticks:* Cut a three-foot dowel into three one-foot sticks. Seven 3-foot dowels make enough sticks for ten players. To play, simply hit one stick against the other. For an extra sound, make grooves on one stick and rub with a smooth stick.

   - *Claves:* Originally, claves were made from the trunks of young trees. For this orchestra, use heavy cardboard tubes. To play, simply hold one tube and hit with the other.

   - *Rhythm Blocks:* Any wood scraps can be cut into rhythm blocks. For an added sound, glue a sheet of medium sandpaper on one side of each block and shuffle off. Each player will need two blocks.

   - *Maracas:* Fill small boxes and paper lunch bags with buttons, beads, marbles, and pebbles. Secure with rubber bands and shake.

2. Each player selects an instrument. Divide the group into three sections. With the leader conducting, ask the first section to beat out a rhythm. While the first section continues, the second section begins to beat out a counter rhythm. Both sections continue as the third section adds another rhythm. Each section takes a turn changing its rhythm while the other sections adjust their tempos accordingly.

3. Divide the group into two orchestras. The two groups face each other. The object is for each orchestra to "talk" to the other using the instruments. Taking turns, one group beats out about 15 or 20 seconds of sound—shaking maracas, hitting rhythm sticks, and rubbing blocks. The other group reacts by playing back, either in a calm even tone or with frantic excitement.

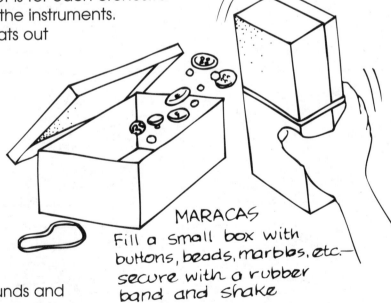

MARACAS
Fill a small box with buttons, beads, marbles, etc.— secure with a rubber band and shake

4. Finish with a big finale using voices and other sounds. It is surprising how well inexperienced musicians can organize sounds and rhythms into a spontaneous symphony.

© McGraw-Hill Children's Publishing

0-7424-1940-1 *The Incredible Indoor Games Book*

Storyboard

Before the actors are hired and the cameras roll, every director presents a storyboard to describe what the movie or TV show will be like. Storyboards resemble comic books because they are a series of pictures that illustrate the story step by step.

Materials needed:

Several sheets of standard-sized paper for each team

A pencil or marker for each player

Room arrangement:

Groups of chairs and tables

Time:

45 minutes

Variation:

Have teams photograph their objects with a digital camera and arrange the pictures in a PowerPoint slide show with captions, sounds, and music.

Directions:

1. Divide the group into smaller teams of three. Give each team a stack of paper and pencils.

2. Each team needs to work together to develop a story called "A Day in the Life of…" a familiar, everyday object such as a pencil, ball, bike, shoe, chair, etc. For example, "A Day in the Life of a Pencil" might describe a discarded pencil that was found on the street, how it found a new home, who used it, what it wrote, and how it felt when put into a pencil sharpener.

3. Once the teams decide on their topics, they draw one picture on each sheet of paper to illustrate a scene in the object's adventures. Sheets should be arranged like a storybook, with a beginning, middle, and ending.

4. After teams have completed their storyboards, they are ready to show off their ideas. Teams may tape sheets across the wall or show each sheet individually. Players may wish to act out the object's thoughts or words with appropriate voices and theatrical gestures.

© McGraw-Hill Children's Publishing   0-7424-1940-1 *The Incredible Indoor Games Book*

Lip Service

This game is similar to Lip Sync except that players record their dubbing on videotape.

Materials needed:

Video camera

VCR

Monitor

Videotape

Room arrangement:

Open space

Time:

25 minutes

Directions:

1. Divide the players into groups of four. Each player should get a turn to play both roles—on-camera actor and off-camera talker.

2. The on-camera players act out a pantomime conversation while the other two players stand off camera and fill in the words.

3. Limit each group to three minutes on camera. After several performances, play the tape.

Dr. Jekyll and Mr. Hyde

Everyone likes to mug for the camera. Sometimes it's hard to get a serious expression. Here's a game where players transform themselves into other creatures right before the camera.

Materials needed:

Video camera

VCR

Monitor

Videotape

Room arrangement:

Open space

Time:

25 minutes

Directions:

1. Dr. Jekyll and Mr. Hyde were actually the same person, but, because of a failed science experiment, the doctor would transform into another person at night and scare townspeople. Players may need to practice their scary Mr. Hyde faces before trying this activity.

2. The leader stands at one end of the room with a video camera. Players line up and take turns looking straight into the camera. They should start out with a serious face and slowly transform into another "creature" by changing their expressions.

3. After everyone in the group has been videotaped, watch the playback. For added silliness, try playing some funny or scary music as a soundtrack. Players can vote for the Dr. Jekyll/Mr. Hyde with the most noticeable difference.

© McGraw-Hill Children's Publishing 0-7424-1940-1 *The Incredible Indoor Games Book*

Paparazzi!

Very famous people try to hide from the cameras when they are caught off-guard. In this video activity, players become famous celebrities who want to avoid being seen at all costs.

Materials needed:

Video camera

VCR

Monitor

Videotape

Room arrangement:

Open space

Time:

25 minutes

Directions:

1. Set video equipment at one end of the room with the camera and monitor facing players. Give players as much room as possible to be active. Players pretend they are very famous people who do not want to be seen by the paparazzi. The object of the game is to try to escape the watchful camera lens without actually hiding behind furniture or objects.

2. Players gather at one end of the room. The leader, standing in one spot, slowly pans the room as the celebrities watch the monitor. Players must try not to be on screen and must rely on fast footwork—ducking, crawling, dodging, and so forth.

3. As players begin to wear themselves out, exhausted celebrities get to see the rerun of the tape. Players can decide who was the most elusive celebrity.

© McGraw-Hill Children's Publishing 0-7424-1940-1 *The Incredible Indoor Games Book*

Earthquake

Players get all shook up as they mimic this geologic fault.

Materials needed:

Video camera

VCR

Monitor

Videotape

Room arrangement:

Open space

Time:

25 minutes

Directions:

1. Set video equipment at one end of the room with monitor facing away from players. Players sit, stand, talk, and act as if nothing were happening.

2. As the videotape is recording the calm activities of the players, the leader yells "Earthquake!" and starts to shake the camera to simulate ground movement. Players react by shaking, falling, and pretending the floor is shifting under them.

3. Play back the tape for the shook-up players.

© McGraw-Hill Children's Publishing
0-7424-1940-1 *The Incredible Indoor Games Book*

Straight Face

It doesn't make sense. When you know you're supposed to laugh, things just don't seem very funny. But things suddenly seem hilarious when you're not allowed to crack a smile. This game records players' abilities to keep a straight face under pressure.

Materials needed:

Video camera

VCR

Monitor

Videotape

Room arrangement:

Open space

Time:

30 minutes

Directions:

1. Set up the camera at one end of the room. Players take turns staring into the camera without cracking a smile—or any expression—for 15 seconds.

2. Off-camera players try to make the stone-face crack a smile. They can make faces or funny gestures, but they may not touch the on-camera player or make any noise. Turn off the camera between takes so that only the serious stares of players will be shown.

3. Play back the videotape so that stone-faced players will have a chance to laugh at themselves.

Funny Faces

Everyone likes to mug for the camera. Here's a game where making a face is the rule and not the exception.

Materials needed:

Video camera

VCR

Monitor

Videotape

Room arrangement:

Open space

Time:

25 minutes

Directions:

1. Players may need some funny-face practice before trying this activity. They can use a mirror to perfect their perfect look.

2. The leader stands at one end of the room with the video camera. Players line up and take turns making their silliest face into the camera.

3. Play back the videotape. For added silliness, play some funny music as a soundtrack. Players can vote for the funniest face.

© McGraw-Hill Children's Publishing 0-7424-1940-1 *The Incredible Indoor Games Book*

Classroom Idol

Everyone has a secret talent to boast about. It doesn't need to be singing and dancing, but it could be some incredible accomplishment or exciting experience. Talents can range from playing a sport to making craft projects. This talent show features everyone's best assets.

Materials needed:

Video camera

VCR

Monitor

Videotape

Room arrangement:

Open space

Time:

30–45 minutes

YOU'RE ON NEXT.

Directions:

1. Set up the camera in front of a blank wall, which will become the TV studio. If you want to get fancy, the group can make a backdrop with rolls of paper, glitter, foil, and paint.

2. Players each get to choose their best talent. It could be playing an instrument, drawing pictures, singing, dancing, writing, figuring out a complicated math problem, or anything else.

3. Since the TV studio is small, this can be run like a talk show, with one player interviewing another. Players introduce themselves and then describe and perform their talent for the interviewer. Keep a time limit on each interview.

4. After everyone has presented her of his talent, play back the tape to show how many terrific people are right in the room. There's no need to judge this one because each person is already a Classroom Idol!

© McGraw-Hill Children's Publishing 0-7424-1940-1 *The Incredible Indoor Games Book*

Tunnels

The easiest of all arches to make is the three-box arch, which, architecturally speaking, isn't actually an arch but a lintel. Whatever it is, it is easy to make and can be made quickly. If many are placed in line, the tunnel is born.

Materials needed:

50 to 75 cardboard boxes

Room arrangement:

Open space

Time:

25 minutes

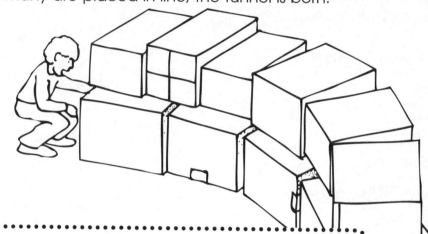

Directions:

1. Close flaps on the boxes by overlapping them. Decide with the group how long and what shape the tunnel should be. Tunnels can be straight or they can wind, spiral, and snake.

2. After some design agreements have been made, players should stack two parallel rows of boxes with enough space between them to crawl through. Then, they can put the boxes on top to cover it. Suggest that players leave some top boxes off for skylights or that they build small individual-sized niches off the main tunnel.

3. Even before the tunnel is finished, players will begin crawling in and out. Be careful, however, of players crawling on top of the tunnel while others are inside.

4. Tunnels can be even more fun when they are connected to secret rooms or other constructions, like fabric-covered tents. Tunnels can be used in other games and activities, such as Follow-the-Leader.

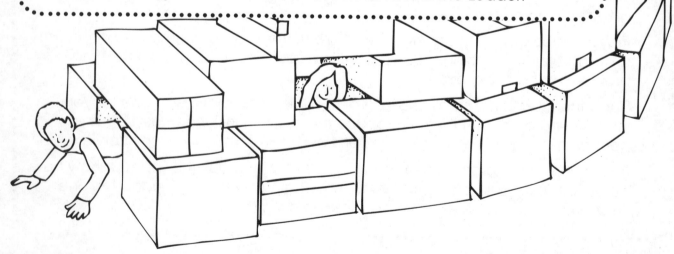

© McGraw-Hill Children's Publishing

0-7424-1940-1 *The Incredible Indoor Games Book*

Box Links

When the flaps of two boxes are joined together, the result is a building unit with infinite possibilities.

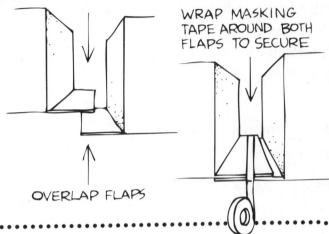

WRAP MASKING TAPE AROUND BOTH FLAPS TO SECURE

OVERLAP FLAPS

Materials needed:

60 to 80 cardboard boxes of various sizes

Masking tape

Room arrangement:

Open space

Time:

30–40 minutes

Directions:

1. Divide players into groups of five or six. Give each group about 15 boxes and a roll of masking tape.

2. In this activity, the flaps of boxes are taped together into a hinge that creates a flip-flop module. To tape flaps, bring two boxes together and overlap flaps. Wrap masking tape around both flaps to secure.

3. Since one box has as many as eight flaps, the possibilities of connecting it to other boxes are endless. Boxes can be connected into a single snaking line, a tank tread, or a complex cluster. Help players get started by demonstrating various possibilities. Two groups might want to work together on one gigantic box chain.

4. When every box has been linked, allow time for everyone to play with the many variations made by the hinges. Box chains might become rocket ships or trains. Changing them into other shapes will take cooperation and some inventive planning. When players seem to be finished with their box constructions, store them for later use.

© McGraw-Hill Children's Publishing 0-7424-1940-1 *The Incredible Indoor Games Book*

Stacking the Deck

Activities are not always defined by rules—some are defined by the materials used. In this activity, players explore materials and the games occur spontaneously. When players stack boxes, far more is happening than is obvious.

Materials needed:

50 to 75 cardboard boxes

Room arrangement:

Open space

Time:

25 minutes

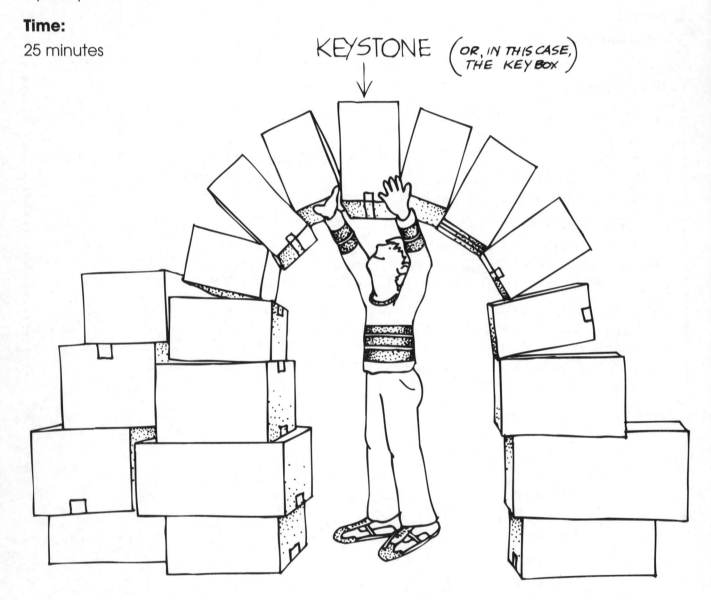

KEYSTONE (OR, IN THIS CASE, THE KEY BOX)

© McGraw-Hill Children's Publishing 0-7424-1940-1 *The Incredible Indoor Games Book*

Stacking the Deck (cont.)

Directions:

1. Close boxes by overlapping flaps. Stack them in a pile in the center of the room.

2. Allow players a short time for an initial investigation. Soon, players will welcome some direction. Organize the activity by suggesting a wall built to divide the room.

3. You can assist building, but players will stack the boxes rapidly and enthusiastically. As the wall is being built, players will be on either side walling in or out other players. Hide-and-seek games will soon occur as players play peek-a-boo through the spaces. Continue to direct the overall structure and encourage self-motivated play by having players build the wall as high as possible.

4. After players have built the wall, it inevitably will be knocked down so the process can begin again. In the interest of safety and box conservation, it is best to anticipate this part of the play cycle. Organize a collapsing game with players slowly taking boxes away from the bottom.

5. When boxes have fallen, quickly reorganize everyone by suggesting a more specific challenge—the creation of a large arch. Making an arch out of boxes demands total cooperation and means understanding the nature of the keystone. The keystone is the central box at the crown of the arch that holds all the other boxes in place. To construct the arch, all players will have to hold boxes in the air until the keystone can be set in place.

6. The success of the cooperative arch will provide a positive atmosphere in which players can organize themselves in other self-motivated projects.

© McGraw-Hill Children's Publishing 0-7424-1940-1 *The Incredible Indoor Games Book*

Boxing Match

There's no fighting in this game—just a creative battle of wits. With this activity, players not only make their own puzzle, but also try to figure out how it fits together.

Materials needed:

9 cardboard boxes

Paint cups

Brushes

Tempera paint in assorted colors

Bucket of water

Sponge or mop

Newspapers

Pencils

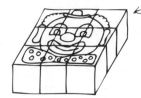

DRAW A DESIGN OVER ALL 9 BOXES

Room arrangement:

Open space

Time:

45 minutes

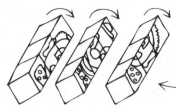

TURN BOXES AND DRAW DESIGNS UNTIL ALL SIDES ARE FILLED

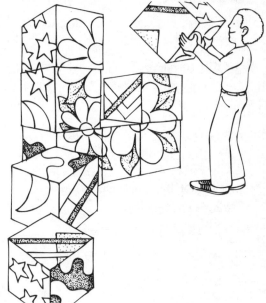

Directions:

1. Divide players into nine groups. Give each group a cardboard box, assorted colors of tempera paint in cups, several brushes, and some newspaper to cover the floor. Keep a bucket of water and a sponge or mop close by for cleanup.

2. Assemble the boxes in the center of the floor, flush against each other in three rows of three. The object of the activity is to draw a large picture on the combined surfaces of all nine boxes. Have players choose a simple design or object to draw—a face, flower, house, or geometric design. Give pencils to two or three players to draw a simple outline of the design over all nine boxes.

3. When the drawing is finished, turn the boxes to a clean side and have two or three different players draw another picture. Repeat the large outline drawings until all six sides of each box have a different design.

4. Next, have each group paint all six sides of its box in any manner it chooses—as long as each outline and design is followed.

5. When paintings are dry, reassemble them into one of the six pictures. Allow players time to rearrange the blocks into the six different pictures or invent new ones by mixing the designs.

© McGraw-Hill Children's Publishing 0-7424-1940-1 *The Incredible Indoor Games Book*

Boxed In

There's nothing square about costumes made from boxes. With a little labor and some imagination, boxes can become robots, cars, birds, and fish. Here are a few box steps to help move players in the right direction.

Materials needed:

Boxes of assorted sizes, one for each player

Utility knife

Newspapers

Masking tape

A pencil or felt-tipped marker for each player

A paint cup for each player

A brush for each player

Miscellaneous pieces of cardboard, small boxes, paper plates, and so forth

Room arrangement:

Open space

Time:

60 minutes

CUT EARS, WINGS AND FINS FROM SCRAP PIECES-- SLOT AND SLIP INTO PLACE

Directions:

1. Before the activity begins, prepare boxes by cutting holes for heads, arms, and bodies. Move furniture to the edges of the room. Protect the floor by covering it with newspaper.

2. Place precut boxes in a pile in the center of the room. Keep paints centrally located at one table, allowing players to take and return one cup of paint at a time.

3. Each player selects a box. Before players begin to paint, discuss box-costume designs, listing an assortment of possibilities, from dragons to flying saucers.

4. Players draw in designs first with pencils—outlining feathers, flowers, lights, scales, or whatever—before filling in with paint. Additional pieces of cardboard, small boxes, and paper plates can be cut and taped on for eyes, heads, feet, wings, tails, and so forth.

5. Completed box costumes can be displayed in a fashion show or can be the basis for improvised skits.

© McGraw-Hill Children's Publishing   0-7424-1940-1 *The Incredible Indoor Games Book*

Amazing Boxes

Mazes are at least as old as the Minotaur myth and as recent as the fun house at the amusement park. People of all ages enjoy the adventure of trying to find their way out of a labyrinth. In this activity, players lose themselves not only in a maze but in the process of building it.

Materials needed:

50 to 75 cardboard boxes of various sizes

Tempera paint in assorted colors

5 brushes for every 3 players

5 paint cups for every 3 players

Bucket of water

Masking tape

A pencil for each player

Newspapers

Room arrangement:

Open space

Time:

45–60 minutes

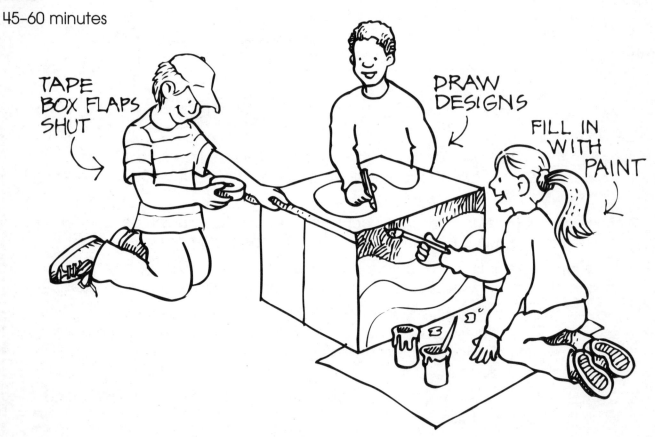

TAPE BOX FLAPS SHUT

DRAW DESIGNS

FILL IN WITH PAINT

© McGraw-Hill Children's Publishing 0-7424-1940-1 *The Incredible Indoor Games Book*

Amazing Boxes (cont.)

Directions:

1. Divide players into groups of three. Give each group several boxes, five cups of paint in various colors, a brush for each color, several pencils, and masking tape to share with other groups. Pass around sheets of newspaper so that players can cover the floor.

2. Before the mazes are created, decorate the boxes with signs and symbols. Directional elements, such as arrows, can be used in the maze to send players in different directions. Words such as *Danger* or *Enter at your own risk!* add mystery to the maze. Other decorative elements such as stars, dots, and patterns can be added for the eye-catching fun of it.

3. When every box is painted and dry, players can arrange the boxes in a maze. Players stack boxes in a confusing network of hidden routes and dead-end passages. Boxes should be piled high enough so that players moving through the maze cannot see other players and cannot tell where the passage leads. Parts of the maze can be enclosed with other boxes to create dark, mysterious chambers.

4. Playing with the maze is the most fun. Older children will enjoy the decorating and the construction while smaller children will be happy just to crawl around. Young children enjoy having you pretend to be a dragon or a monster.

5. After this activity, store the decorated boxes for fast fun—over and over again.

© McGraw-Hill Children's Publishing   0-7424-1940-1 *The Incredible Indoor Games Book*

Nice Big Dice

The making of very big dice leads to the creation of very big games with very big stakes.

Materials needed:

2 cube-shaped cardboard boxes of similar size

Masking tape

Black felt-tipped marker

Room arrangement:

Open space

Time:

30 minutes

I'M READY!

Directions:

1. Tape box flaps securely shut with masking tape. Add dots with a black felt-tipped marker. On a traditional die, the numbers on opposite faces always add up to seven. (If you would like to make fancy dice, paint the boxes with white acrylic before applying dots.)

2. To throw oversized dice, clear the area. On the count of three, toss. One player is generally needed to toss each die. Big dice are very theatrical and can make any game in which dice are required a special game.

Chip Off the Old Block

1. If lots of boxes have been collected for other activities, use them as big playing "chips."

2. Divide the group into two teams.

3. When a team rolls a seven or a double, that team gets a chip. A team that gets an eleven must forfeit one chip to the other team.

4. The team that collects all the chips is the winner.

© McGraw-Hill Children's Publishing 0-7424-1940-1 *The Incredible Indoor Games Book*

Nice Big Dice (cont.)

Ten Steps

1. Divide the group into two teams—one "odd" and the other "even."

2. Divide the room in half with a line of masking tape on the floor.

3. Have each team line up ten steps behind its side of the line.

4. If the odd team throws 3, 5, 7, 9, or 11, all odd-team members take one step forward. If the even team throws 4, 6, 8, 10, or 12, all even-team members take one step forward. If odd throws even or even throws odd, nobody moves. If either team throws a 2 (snake eyes), team members must each retreat one step.

5. The first team to reach the center line is the winner.

54

1. This game requires two teams of 15 players. Each team gets one die. The object is to throw the die 15 times (each player throws once) and get 54 points or as close as possible to 54 without going over. (If there are 20 players, change the game to two teams of players, 10 throws and 36 points.)

2. Both teams stand in line. The leader says "Go" and the first player on each team throws his or her die into the center of the room. All players take a turn throwing their team's die.

3. Scores are added up. If a team gets 55 or more points, it loses. If the teams tie, they both win.

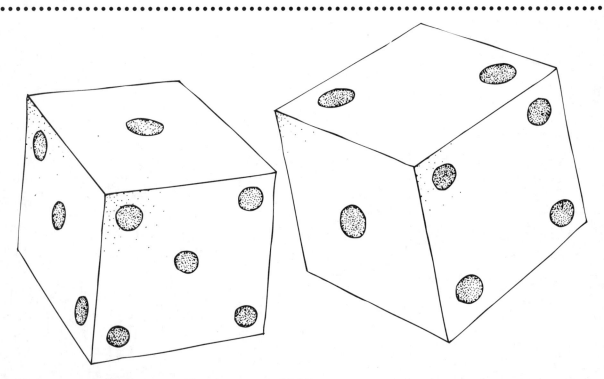

© McGraw-Hill Children's Publishing   0-7424-1940-1 *The Incredible Indoor Games Book*

Shoe-Box Dominoes

In the traditional game of dominoes, players try to match the number of dots on one tile with the number of dots on another. While serious domino players in one room are mulling over their moves, others are in another room building a long line of dominoes standing on end, giving the last one in line a little nudge, and enjoying the spectacle of a domino chain reaction as the tiles topple. This game replaces the small domino tiles with a shoe-box spectacular.

Materials needed:

As many shoe boxes as possible (at least 100)

Newspapers

Tempera paint in assorted colors

A paint cup for each player

A brush for each player

Masking tape

Room arrangement:

Open space

Time:

60 minutes

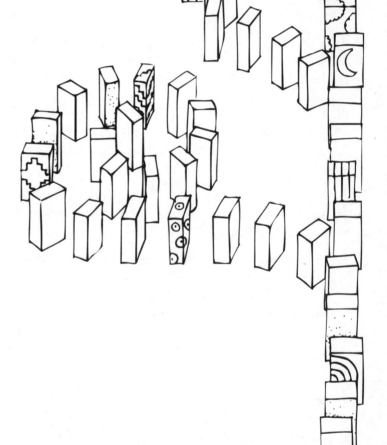

© McGraw-Hill Children's Publishing

0-7424-1940-1 *The Incredible Indoor Games Book*

Shoe-Box Dominoes (cont.)

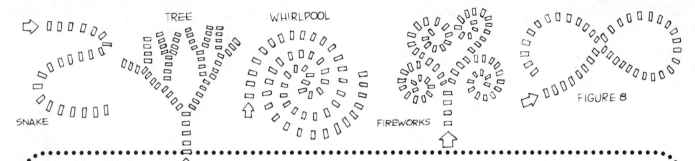

SNAKE   TREE   WHIRLPOOL   FIREWORKS   FIGURE 8

Directions:

1. Ask everyone in the group to help collect shoe boxes for this spectacular.

2. Since this is not a traditional domino game, shoe boxes can be decorated with all kinds of colors and designs. First, tape box tops to box bottoms. To decorate, separate the players into three teams with equal numbers of shoe boxes. Divide paint supplies among the teams. Each person can paint one box at a time or players can pass the boxes down an assembly line on newspaper sheets with each person adding one small design.

3. Once all boxes are dry, it's time to test out some falling formations.

   • Snake: The Snake is the most basic. Stand boxes on end in a curving line. Boxes on the inside of the turn almost touch each other to insure proper toppling

   • Tree: The Tree is a line of boxes that branches off into more lines. Having one box hit two other boxes will set off two other lines. Each of those lines can split off into other lines, and so forth.

   • Whirlpool: The Whirlpool is a double spiral. To create a spiral, turn boxes in a continuous curve that gets smaller toward the center. At the center, turn the spiral out in reverse, placing the reverse spiral between the lines of the other spiral. Some adjustment may have to be made to leave room between the lines.

   • Fireworks: Fireworks uses spirals combined with a Tree. Begin with a straight line at the end of which one box hits two other boxes. The two boxes set off two spirals. More Fireworks can be added by having spirals branch off other spirals.

   • Figure 8: In the Figure 8, the shoe-box lines crisscross. Where one line crosses another, be sure to leave a large enough gap so that falling boxes do not accidentally hit the intersecting line.

4. After a few trial runs and some experimentation with some other formations, everyone should be ready for the Giant Shoe-Box Domino Spectacular. Have each group set up a domino design, curving boxes around furniture and under tables and twisting lines into geometric patterns. Groups should find ways to connect their designs into one big domino fall. Draw a name for the Official Shoe-Box Toppler and then have a mass countdown.

© McGraw-Hill Children's Publishing   0-7424-1940-1 *The Incredible Indoor Games Book*

Fun City

This may be the only opportunity students will have to design a world where having fun is the only job.

Materials needed:

6 to 10 appliance boxes (from refrigerators, washing machines, and so forth)

Felt-tipped markers

Tempera paint in assorted colors

A paint cup for each player

A brush for each player

Bucket of water

Newspaper

Room arrangement:

Open space

Time:

60 minutes

Directions:

1. Clear the room of furniture and cover the floor with newspapers. Arrange boxes around the edges of the room, leaving enough space for construction. Collect paint supplies at one table.

2. With the group seated, discuss ways to design a city as if it was an amusement park and the major industry was having fun. Decide on the theme and the fun-making attributes of each box. For example, one box might be called Free Jokes, with a player hidden inside ready to pop out with a joke. Other boxes might be filled with strange sounds, small holes for peeking, free fortunes, or a House of Horrors.

3. Divide the group into groups of three or four for each themed box. After agreeing on the design, players should begin to outline doors, windows, and any other opening that needs to be cut. (An adult should cut openings with a utility knife.)

4. Have players take a brush and one cup of paint at a time and return to the paint table for refills and for other colors. They can clean paint-soaked brushes in the bucket of water.

5. As the residents of Fun City finish decorating their fun buildings with bright colors and whimsical designs, move the boxes into place. When the paint is dry, have the "Funites" (as the occupants are called) get to work having fun.

© McGraw-Hill Children's Publishing   0-7424-1940-1 *The Incredible Indoor Games Book*